D0721234

DAY
&OVERNIGHT HIKES

Great Smoky
Mountains

N A T I O N A L   P A R K

Other Books by Johnny Molloy

Visit the author's Web site:

www.johnnymolloy.com

Great Smoky
Mountains

NATIONAL PARK

THIRD EDITION

JOHNNY MOLLOY

MENASHA RIDGE PRESS

Copyright © 1995, 2001, 2004 by Johnny Molloy

Published by Menasha Ridge Press
Printed in Canada
Distributed by The Globe Pequot Press
Third edition, first printing, 2004

Text and cover design by Palace Press International
Cover photograph by Karl Weatherly © Getty Images
Author photograph © Lisa Daniel
Typesetting by Annie Long
Maps and elevation profiles by Scott McGrew and Steve Jones

Cataloging-in-Publication Data
Molloy, Johnny, 1961–
Day and overnight hikes in the Great Smoky Mountains
National Park/by Johnny Molloy.–3rd. ed.
p.cm.

ISBN 0-89732-560-5

1. Hiking—Great Smoky Mountains National Park (N.C.
and Tenn.)—Guidebooks. 2. Backpacking—Great Smoky
Mountains National Park (N.C. and Tenn.)—Guidebooks.
3. Trails—Great Smoky Mountains National Park (N.C. and
Tenn.)—Guidebooks. 4. Great Smoky Mountans National
Park (N.C. and Tenn.)—Guidebooks. I. Title.

GV199.42.G73M6 2004
917.68'890454–dc22

Menasha Ridge Press
P.O. Box 43673
Birmingham, Alabama 35243
www.menasharidge.com

Table of Contents

Part I: Great Out and Backs

TENNESSEE

NORTH CAROLINA

Part II: Great Day Loops

Part III: Great Overnight Loops

Dedication

This book is for Lisa Ann Daniel, who needs to take a hike.

Acknowledgments

Most books have only one person's name below the title—the author's. But this book, as others, took a group effort to complete. First and foremost, I would like to thank Teresa Ann McSpurren for developing the idea while we were on a canoe trip in British Columbia. A Canadian, she had come to the Smokies often in her youth and loves them dearly. We met there and have remained friends ever since.

Thanks to Meredith Morris-Babb for steering me in the right direction, and to Mike Jones, Bud Zehmer, Nathan Lott, and the rest of the folks at Menasha Ridge Press. I would be remiss not to thank W. W. Armstrong, Jennifer Dyer, Nancy McBee, and my niece Jill Molloy for their help as well. Thanks to Aaron Marable for going on the latest Smokies hikes, too.

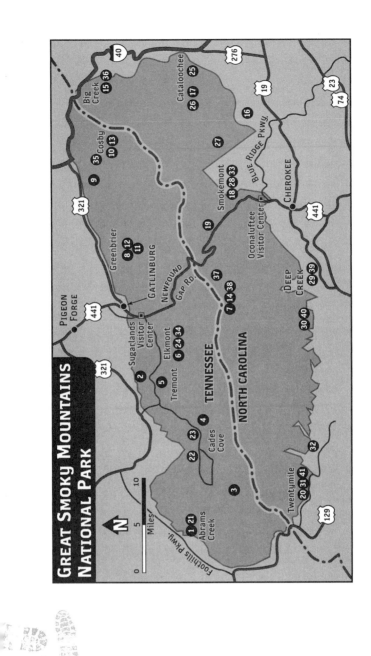

GREAT SMOKY MOUNTAINS NATIONAL PARK

viii

Map Key

Preface

THE GREAT SMOKY MOUNTAINS National Park: 270 miles of roads, 850 miles of trails, 500,000 acres of land. The numbers of flora and fauna are just as impressive: 50 species of mammals, 80 species of fish, 200 species of birds, 1,300 species of flowering plants, 2,000 species of fungi, and more. The park boasts seven trees of record dimensions among the upwards of 130 species that grow here. The diversity of ecosystems found in the Smokies is unmatched by any other temperate climate. Perhaps this is the reason for their impressive designation as both a national park and an international biosphere reserve.

To choose the Smokies as a place to spend your free time is a wise decision. And yet the Smokies can be intimidating, especially for the first-time visitor. Not only is there a lot of land to see, but with more than 9 million guests annually, the Great Smoky Mountains National Park is the most visited national park in the American system. Quite intimidating indeed. Thus, this book was conceived to make the real majesty of the Smokies accessible to visitors.

With so much land and so many people, discovering the beauty and solitude of this national park seems a hit-or-miss proposition. Where are the spectacular vistas? Where are the waterfalls and the old settlers' cabins? Where can I find solitude? Leaving it all to chance doesn't offer good odds for your all-too-brief vacation from the rat race. Weeks spent daydreaming of your fleeting slice of freedom could culminate in a three-hour driving marathon or a noisy walk up a crowded trail. Fortunately, with a little bit of planning and forethought, and this book, you can make the most of your time in the Smokies.

This book presents more than 30 day hikes for you to choose from. The majority of the hikes steer you toward infrequently visited areas, giving you the opportunity to enjoy your vacation on the trail instead of behind someone's car. These hikes offer solitude to maximize your Smoky Mountains experience but by necessity portions of some hikes traverse popular and potentially crowded areas.

The day hikes offered here fall into one of two categories: out-and-back or loop. Out-and-back hikes take you to a particular rewarding destination and back on the same trail. The return trip allows you to see everything from the opposite vantage point. You may notice more minute features the second go-round, and retracing your steps at a different time of day can give the same trail a surprisingly different character.

To some, however, a return trip on the same trail isn't as enjoyable. Some hikers just can't stand the thought of covering the same ground twice, not with hundreds of untrodden Smokies miles awaiting them. Loop hikes avoid this. The loop hikes in this book are generally longer and harder than the out-and-back hikes, but a bigger challenge can reap bigger rewards.

Day hiking is the best and most popular way to "break into" the Smokies backcountry, but for those with the inclination, this book also offers ten overnight hikes. There are 102 designated backcountry sites and shelters available for those who want to capture the changing moods of the mountains. The length of these hikes, three days and two nights, accommodates those who have only an extended weekend. Longer trips are also available for those with more time. A permit is required for overnight stays in the backcountry. Certain campsites may be reserved in advance. Permits are available at visitor centers or by calling (865) 436-1231.

When visiting the Smokies, it's a great temptation to remain in your car, in part because auto tours, including one end of the famed Blue

Ridge Parkway, abound. While auto touring is a great way to get an overview of the park, it creates a barrier between you and the mountains. Windshield tourists, hoping for a glimpse of bears and other wildlife, often end up seeing the tail end of the car in front of them. And while roadside overlooks offer easy views, the drone of traffic and lack of effort in reaching the views can make them less than inspirational. The Smokies were made for hiking.

The wilderness experience can unleash your mind and body, allowing you to relax and find peace and quiet. It also enables you to catch glimpses of beauty and splendor: a deer crashing through the underbrush as it clambers up a mountainside; the cabin remains of early settlers who scrabbled out a living among these woods; or a spectacular waterfall crashing above and below a trail. Out in these woods you can let your mind roam free, go where it pleases. This can't be achieved in a climate-controlled automobile.

The next few sections offer advice on how to use this book and how to have a safe and pleasant hike in the woods. The Smokies are a wild and beautiful place. I hope you will get out and enjoy what they have to offer.

—*Johnny Molloy*

Introduction

How to Use This Guidebook

AT THE TOP OF EACH hike profile is an information box that allows the hiker quick access to pertinent information: quality of scenery, difficulty of hike, condition of trail, expected degree of solitude, appropriateness for children, as well as distance, approximate duration, and some highlights of the trip. The first five categories are rated using a five-star system. Below is an example of a box included with a hike:

Twentymile Loop

SCENERY: ✿ ✿ ✿ ✿
DIFFICULTY: ✿ ✿
TRAIL CONDITION: ✿ ✿ ✿
SOLITUDE: ✿ ✿ ✿ ✿ ✿
CHILDREN: ✿ ✿ ✿ ✿
DISTANCE: *7.4 miles round-trip*
HIKING TIME: *3:45 round-trip*
OUTSTANDING FEATURES: *waterfall, mountain streams, deep woods*

On this hike, four stars indicate that scenery will be picturesque, it will be a relatively easy climb (five stars for difficulty would be strenuous), the trail conditions are average (one star means the trail is likely to be muddy, narrow, or have some obstacle), you can expect to run into few if any people (with one star you'll likely be elbowing your way up the trail), and the hike is appropriate for able-bodied children (a one-star rating would denote that only the most gung-ho and physically fit children should go).

The distance is absolute, but the hiking time is an estimate for the average hiker making a round-trip. Overnight hiking times factor in the burden of carrying a pack.

Following each box is a brief description of the hike. A more detailed account follows, noting trail junctions, stream crossings, and trailside features, along with their distances from the trail-head. This helps to keep you apprised of your whereabouts and makes sure you don't miss those features noted. You can use this guidebook to walk just a portion of a hike or to combine information to plan a hike of your own.

The hikes have been divided into Out-and-Back Day Hikes, Loop Day Hikes, and Overnight Loops. The Day Hikes sections have been further divided into Tennessee and North Carolina hikes. Feel free to flip through the book, reading the descriptions and choosing a hike that appeals to you.

Weather

The Smoky Mountains offer four distinct seasons for the hiker's enjoyment, but sometimes it seems all four are going on at once, depending on your location and elevation. Before your visit is over, you will probably see a little bit of everything.

Be prepared for a wide range of temperatures and conditions, no matter the season. As a rule of thumb, the temperature decreases about three degrees with every 1,000 feet of elevation gained. The Smokies are also the wettest place in the South. The park's higher elevations can receive upwards of 90 inches of precipitation a year.

Spring, the most variable season, takes six weeks to reach the park's highest elevations. You may encounter both winter- and summer-like weather during April and May, often in the same day. As the weather warms, thunderstorms become more frequent. Summer days typically start clear, but as the day heats up, clouds build, often culminating in a heavy shower. Fall, the driest season, comes to the peaks in early September, working its way downhill, the reverse pattern of spring; warm days and cool nights are interspersed with less-frequent wet periods.

Winter presents the Smokies at their most challenging. Frontal systems sweep through the region, with alternately cloudy and sunny days, though cloudy days are most frequent. No permanent snow pack exists in the high country, though areas over 5,000 feet receive five feet of snow or more per year. The high country can see bitterly cold temperature readings during this time. When venturing in the Smokies, it's a good idea to carry clothes for all weather extremes.

Clothing

There is a wide variety of materials to choose from. Basically, use common sense and be prepared for anything. If all you have are cotton clothes when a sudden rainstorm comes along, you'll get miserable quickly, especially in cooler weather. It's a good idea to carry along a light wool sweater or some type of synthetic apparel (Capilene®, Thermax®, etc.) as well as a hat. A poncho or other rain gear (GORE-TEX®, etc.) is appropriate too.

Footwear is another concern. Though tennis shoes may be appropriate in paved areas, the majority of the trails can be uneven and rough; tennis shoes may not offer enough support. Boots, waterproof or not, are the footwear of choice. Sport sandals are increasingly popular, but these leave much of your foot exposed. A sliced foot far from the trailhead can make for a miserable limp back to the car.

Safety Concerns

To some potential mountain enthusiasts, the deep woods seem inordinately dark, perilous, and full of hazards. It is the fear of the unknown that causes this anxiety. No doubt, potentially dangerous situations can occur in the outdoors, but as long as you use sound judgment and prepare yourself before you hit the trail, you'll be much safer in the woods than in most urban areas in our country. It is better to look at a backcountry hike as a fascinating discovery of the unknown, rather than a potential for disaster. Here are a few tips to make your trip safer and easier:

• Always bring food and water, even when day hiking. Food will give you energy, help keep you warm, and in an emergency situation may sustain you until help arrives. And you never know if you will find a stream nearby when you are thirsty. Of course, if you drink water from a stream, purify it first. The chance of getting sick from the organism known as giardia or other waterborne organisms is small, but there is no reason to take a chance. Boil, filter, or treat all water before drinking it. Outdoor retailers offer a wide range of water filters and purification tablets.

• Stay on designated trails. Most hikers get lost when they leave the trail. If you become disoriented, don't panic—this may result in a bad decision that will make your predicament worse. Retrace your steps if you can remember them, or stay put. Rangers check the trails first when searching for lost or overdue hikers.

• Bring a map, compass, and lighter, and know how to use a map and compass. Should you become lost, these three items can help you stick around long enough to be found or get yourself out of a pickle. Trail maps are available at visitor centers and ranger stations. A compass can help you orient yourself, and a lighter can start a fire (for heat or for signaling).

• Be especially careful crossing streams. Whether you are fording or crossing on a footlog, make every step count. If using a footlog, hold onto the handrail, and be aware that footlogs are often moss covered and slippery. When fording a stream, use a trekking pole or stout limb as a third leg for balance. If a stream seems too high to ford, turn back.

• Be aware of the symptoms of hypothermia. Shivering and forgetfulness are the two most prevalent indicators of this cold-weather killer, which can occur even in the summer at higher elevations, especially when a hiker is wearing wet clothing If symptoms arise, find the victim warm shelter, hot liquids, and dry clothes or a sleeping bag.

• Avoid bear-fear paralysis. The black bears of the Smokies are wild animals, hence unpredictable. If you see one, give it a wide berth; don't feed it and you'll be fine. There are no records of anyone being killed by a bear in the Smokies; most injuries have occurred when an ignorant visitor fed or otherwise harassed a wild bear.

• Always bring rain gear. The Smokies are the wettest place in the East, which is an important factor in the Smokies' remarkable biodiversity. Keep in mind that a rainy day is as much a part of nature as those idyllic ones you desire; and rainy days tend to cut down on the crowds. With the appropriate rain gear, a normally crowded trail can be a place of solitude. Do remember that getting wet opens the door to hypothermia.

• Take along your brain. A cool, calculating mind is the single most important piece of equipment you'll ever need on the trail. Think before you act. Watch your step. Plan ahead. Avoiding accidents before they happen is the best recipe for a rewarding, stress-relieving hike.

• Ask questions. Park employees are there to help. It's a lot easier to gain advice beforehand rather than have a mishap away from civilization, when it's too late to amend an error. Use your head out there, and treat the place as if it were your own backyard. After all, it is your national park.

Tips for Enjoying Smoky Mountains National Park

Before you go, call the national park for an information kit at (865) 436-1200. This will help get you oriented to the roads, features, and attractions of the Smokies. Another helpful source of information is the Great Smoky Mountains National Park Web site: www.nps.gov/grsm.

The following tips will make your visit enjoyable and more rewarding:

• Get out of your car and onto a trail. Auto touring merely allows a cursory overview of the park, and only from a visual perspective. On the trail you can use your ears and nose as well. This guidebook recommends some trails over others, but any trail is better than no trail.

• Use outlying trailheads to start a hike. First, you will avoid the traffic of the main roads. Second, you're more likely to encounter solitude on the outlying trails than on trails off the main roads. The Smokies are big, yet most visitors congregate in a few areas, so branch out.

• Investigate different areas of the park. The Smokies offer a wide variety of elevation, terrain, and forest types. You'll be pleasantly surprised to see so many distinct landscapes in one national park. Detailed USGS maps are on sale at the visitor centers.

• Take your time along the trails. Pace yourself. The Smokies are filled with wonders both big and small. Don't rush past a unique salamander to get to that overlook. Stop and smell the wildflowers. Listen to the woods around you. Peer into the clear mountain stream. Don't miss the trees for the forest.

• We can't always schedule our free time when we want, but try to hike during the week and avoid the traditional holidays if possible. Trails that are packed in the summer are often clear during the colder seasons. If you are hiking on busy days, go early in the morning; it'll enhance your chances of seeing wildlife, too. The trails really clear out during rainy times. However, don't hike during a thunderstorm.

IMPORTANT SMOKIES PHONE NUMBERS

PARK HEADQUARTERS: *(865) 436-1200*

PARK NATURAL HISTORY ASSOCIATION: *(865) 436-0120*

DEVELOPED CAMPING RESERVATIONS: *(800) 365-2267*

BACKCOUNTRY INFORMATION: *(865) 436-1297*

BACKCOUNTRY CAMPING RESERVATIONS: *(865) 436-1231*

part one
GREAT OUT AND BACKS

1

The return trip to the AT will get you huffing and puffing, while thinking of all the people that skipped this second view as is evidenced by the much less used trail tread.

Abrams Falls
from Abrams Creek Ranger Station

SCENERY: ✪ ✪ ✪ ✪ ✪

DIFFICULTY: ✪ ✪

TRAIL CONDITIONS: ✪ ✪ ✪

SOLITUDE: ✪ ✪ ✪

CHILDREN: ✪ ✪ ✪

DISTANCE: *9.8 miles round-trip*

HIKING TIME: *5:30 round-trip*

OUTSTANDING FEATURES: *Abrams Creek gorge, Abrams Falls*

IT'S HARD TO BELIEVE *how few people you'll see going this way to such a popular destination as Abrams Falls. The sounds of Abrams Creek will keep you company for most of the hike, though. This hike starts on the Cooper Road Trail at the back of the Abrams Creek campground. Follow this jeep road through a hemlock forest and across Kingfisher Creek, which can be a wet crossing in high water. At mile 0.9, turn right onto the Little Bottoms Trail, which is hardly more than a glorified manway, as opposed to the wide jeep road that is Cooper Road Trail.*

🏃 Begin a short but steep climb. After topping a small ridge, descend a short distance beyond the ridgetop. In a clearing on your right, between two of the area's many pine trees, you will find a spectacular view. On the trail's right, the gorge of Abrams Creek lines up with the Smokies crest as a backdrop, allowing a view from creek bottom to mountaintop. Continue winding down until you come to the creek. Cross several small branches along Abrams Creek, reaching Little Bottoms Backcountry Campsite #17 at mile 2.5.

Watch your step on this spare trail as it once again climbs the steep side of the gorge filled with the rumblings of Abrams Creek below. Winding in and out of small side hollows, it intersects the Hatcher Mountain Trail at mile 3.1. Keep forward, descending briefly, to intersect the Abrams Falls Trail at mile 3.3.

To the right, the Hannah Mountain Trail begins with a difficult ford of Abrams Creek. As you continue forward along Abrams Creek—

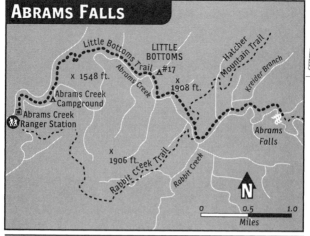

ABRAMS FALLS

ELEVATION PROFILE

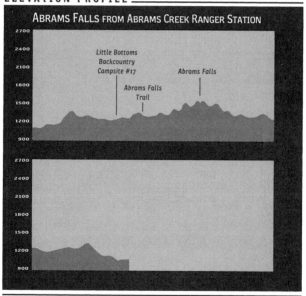

alternately crossing small creeks and looping around rib ridges on a footpath wider than the Little Bottoms Trail—Abrams Creek is always within earshot. At mile 4.9, arrive at the falls. You will see surprising crowds who have come 2.5 miles from Cades Cove. Enjoy the falls and the immense plunge pool before returning to the Abrams Creek Ranger Station.

Walker Sisters Place
via Little Greenbrier Trail

SCENERY: ✿ ✿ ✿ ✿ ✿
DIFFICULTY: ✿ ✿
TRAIL CONDITIONS: ✿ ✿ ✿ ✿
SOLITUDE: ✿ ✿ ✿ ✿
CHILDREN: ✿ ✿ ✿ ✿
DISTANCE: *5.0 miles round-trip*
HIKING TIME: *2:45 round-trip*
OUTSTANDING FEATURES: *views, pioneer homestead*

THIS SCENIC HIKE ALONG A RIDGELINE *offers views down to one of the last working pioneer homesteads in the Smokies. Start at a gap on the Little Greenbrier Trail along the national park boundary. The views are numerous from a pine-cloaked mountainside before reaching a second gap. Dip down to a hollow and reach the Walker Sisters Place, which was occupied by spinster siblings until 1964.*

🏃 Begin this hike at Wear Cove Gap on the Little Greenbrier Trail. Climb through a classic pine-oak forest on a narrow pathway. This path skirts the park border in several places—you will see boundary signs here and there. Also, look down at the elaborate stone work by trail makers that keeps the path from tilting sideways with the mountainside.

Level out in a gap at 0.8 mile, then begin to swing around the south side of Little Mountain. There are good views into the heart of the park. Numerous dead pine snags are the result of the natural relationship between pines and the native pine beetle. There are also views into Wear Cove to the north and Cove Mountain to the east.

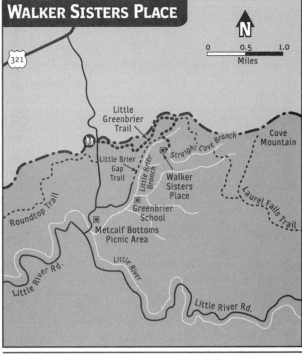

WALKER SISTERS PLACE

321

N

0   0.5   1.0
Miles

Little Greenbrier Trail

Straight Cove Branch

Cove Mountain

Little Brier Gap Trail

Little Brier Branch

Walker Sisters Place

Roundtop Trail

Greenbrier School

Metcalf Bottoms Picnic Area

Little River Rd.

Little River

Little River Rd.

Laurel Falls Trail

TENNESSEE

&OVERNIGHT DAY HIKES

part one
OUT AND BACK

ELEVATION PROFILE

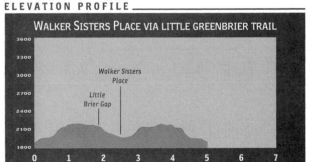

WALKER SISTERS PLACE VIA LITTLE GREENBRIER TRAIL

3600
3300
3000   Walker Sisters Place
2700   Little Brier Gap
2400
2100
1800
      0   1   2   3   4   5   6   7

Drop down the ridge of Little Mountain to reach Little Brier Gap and a trail junction at mile 1.9. Turn right here, on the Little Brier Gap Trail, descending into the moist cove of Little Brier Branch, which lies to your left. Hemlock and tulip trees join the forest. Pass a flat and a former clearing on the left.

Reach a gravel road at 2.3 miles and turn left, along tiny Straight Cove Branch. Come to an open area at 2.5 miles and reach the Walker Sisters Place in a grassy clearing. This cove was occupied for 150 years, with the Walker sisters remaining after the national park was established, thanks to a lifetime lease agreement. After they passed away, the park preserved their homestead. Now, the springhouse, main home, and small barn remain. Notice the notched-log construction of the buildings and the non-native ornamental bushes. If you are further interested in the area's history, continue down the Little Brier Gap Trail for 1.1 more miles to the Little Greenbrier Schoolhouse before returning to Wear Cove Gap.

DIRECTIONS: From the park entrance at Townsend, head forward to the Townsend "Wye." Turn left here, onto Little River Road, and follow it for 7.8 miles to Metcalf Bottoms Picnic Area. Turn left into Metcalf Bottoms Picnic Area, crossing the Little River on a bridge. Keep on the road for 1.3 miles to the park border, where the Little Greenbrier Trail starts on the right. There is parking here for only one car directly by the trail; another parking area is just over the hill from the trailhead.

Gregory Bald *via Gregory Ridge*

SCENERY: ✿ ✿ ✿ ✿ ✿
DIFFICULTY: ✿ ✿ ✿
TRAIL CONDITIONS: ✿ ✿ ✿ ✿
SOLITUDE: ✿ ✿ ✿
CHILDREN: ✿ ✿ ✿
DISTANCE: *10.8 miles round-trip*
HIKING TIME: *5:45 round-trip*
OUTSTANDING FEATURES: *Gregory Bald, views from grassy field, virgin forest*

THIS HIKE IS PACKED WITH FEATURES *to satisfy even the most demanding hiker. On the way to Gregory Bald, world renowned for its wildflowers, pass along a mountain stream surrounded by old growth woodland, ascend a ridge, then pass historic Moore Spring, where an Appalachian Trail shelter once stood. It's a steady climb to the bald but well worth it.*

MAP

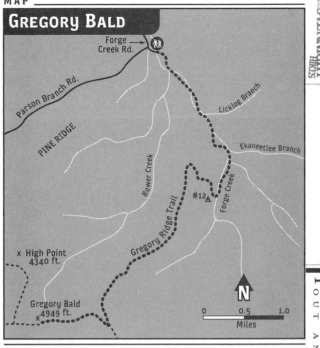

ELEVATION PROFILE

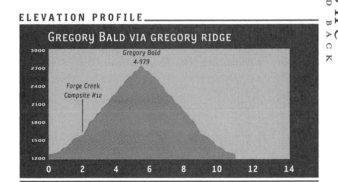

Ascend quickly upon leaving Forge Creek Road to join up with Forge Creek proper, crossing it on a footbridge. A little more than a mile into the hike, an old growth forest of tulip trees and hemlocks begins to dominate the mountain scenery. Tulip trees, formerly known as tulip poplars or just poplars, have been renamed, since they are not true poplars. Footlogs help you cross Forge Creek at miles 1.7 and 1.9. Just

Ascend quickly upon leaving Forge Creek Road to join up with Forge Creek proper, crossing it on a footbridge. A little more than a mile into the hike, an old growth forest of tulip trees and hemlocks begins to dominate the mountain scenery. Tulip trees, formerly known as tulip poplars or just poplars, have been renamed, since they are not true poplars. Footlogs help you cross Forge Creek at miles 1.7 and 1.9. Just beyond the last crossing is Forge Creek Back-country Campsite #12. Fill up with water here, as the rest of the way is dry until Moore Spring.

Leave the valley behind for the drier slope of Gregory Ridge. Top out on the ridge at mile 3.0. You've worked hard to get here, but the ridge keeps on rising. Views of the Smokies to your left keep your spirits up as you near Rich Gap and a trail junction, which lies at mile 4.9.

Here, you will turn right on the Gregory Bald Trail for the final 0.5-mile ascent to Gregory Bald. But first, follow the unmarked path straight ahead. To the left 0.1 mile on, the Long Hungry Ridge Trail from Twenty-Mile Ranger Station terminates. Continue straight for another 0.2 mile to reach Moore Spring, where an Appalachian Trail shelter once stood before the A.T. was rerouted over Fontana Dam in the 1940s. The spring, in a small clearing that beckons you to stop, is one of the Smokies' finest. Remember to treat all water before drinking.

Return to Rich Gap and the trail junction. Turn left on the Gregory Bald Trail, and soon you'll be on the bald, at mile 5.4. Earlier in this century, cattle grazing kept the forest from over-taking this hilltop clearing, or bald, and main-tained a 15-acre open space. By the mid-1980s, the clearing had shrunk to less than half that size. The park service decided to return the Gregory Bald to its original size. Nowadays, don't be surprised if you see the park service actually mowing and cutting back growth at the bald's edges. However, many of the flame azalea bushes are left intact to bloom profusely during June. A hungry hiker can also sample the blueberries later in the summer. Except in inclement weather, Gregory Bald offers nearly 360-degree views year-round. Just a mile west is Parson Bald. To the south are the mountains of the Nantahala National Forest. Cades Cove lies below to the north, with East Tennessee and the Cumberland Mountains beyond.

Rocky Top *via Lead Cove*

SCENERY: ✪ ✪ ✪ ✪ ✪

DIFFICULTY: ✪ ✪ ✪ ✪

TRAIL CONDITIONS: ✪ ✪ ✪ ✪

SOLITUDE: ✪ ✪ ✪ ✪

CHILDREN: ✪ ✪

DISTANCE: *11.4 miles round-trip*

HIKING TIME: *6:00 round-trip*

OUTSTANDING FEATURES: *Spence Field, 360-degree view from Rocky Top*

THIS HIKE IS THE EPITOME OF THE OLD ADAGE, *"You reap what you sow."* You will burn a lot of calories on the climb to your destination, but the view is as good as views get. Leave the lowlands via Lead Cove to intersect Bote Mountain Trail up to the Appalachian Trail, pass through Spence Field, and climb farther still to the storied Rocky Top.

🏃 Leave Laurel Creek Road behind and step into history on the Lead Cove Trail, for what is a hike in the Smokies without a little history? Lead Cove derived its name from the ore that was extracted here in the 1800s. Soon you pass an old homesite that lingers among the cool forest of the cove. Keep climbing somewhat steeply, leaving the bottomland behind to arrive at Sandy Gap and the Bote Mountain Trail at mile 1.8.

Turn right on the ridge-running jeep trail to Bote Mountain. Ascend steadily through the fairly open pine-oak forest that allows intermittent views of Defeat Ridge to your left. At mile 3.0, you'll pass through the Anthony Creek Trail junction, then come to a jeep turnaround at mile 3.7. The trail becomes furrowed and narrow, passing through a seemingly continuous rhododendron tunnel to arrive at a saddle on Spence Field at mile 4.7.

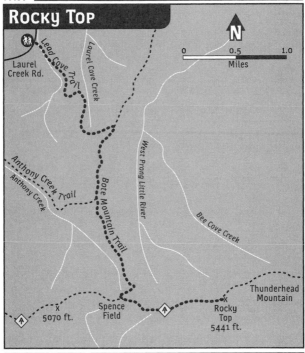

ROCKY TOP

Laurel
Creek Rd.

Lead Cove Tra'l

Laurel Cove Creek

West Prong Little River

Anthony Creek Trail

Anthony Creek

Bote Mountain Trail

Bee Cove Creek

0   0.5   1.0
Miles

N

x
5070 ft.

Spence
Field

Rocky
Top
5441 ft.

Thunderhead
Mountain

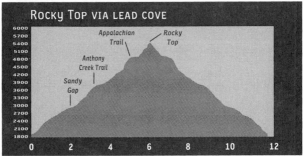

ROCKY TOP VIA LEAD COVE

Appalachian
Trail

Rocky
Top

Anthony
Creek Trail

Sandy
Gap

6000
5700
5400
5100
4800
4500
4200
3900
3600
3300
3000
2700
2400
2100
1800

0   2   4   6   8   10   12

Turn left on the famed Appalachian Trail, skirting Spence Field's eastern flank. Continue alongside the grassy meadow, passing the Jenkins Ridge Trail at mile 5.1. You'll descend briefly only to begin the final 0.6-mile climb to Rocky Top (elevation 5,441 feet) and its awesome views. Once at the summit, you'll understand why the view inspired the famed country song "Rocky Top." The tune doubles as fight song for the

University of Tennessee, which lies a mere 30
miles to the northwest. To your west, the meadows of Spence Field and the western crest of the
Smokies, all the way to Shuckstack Mountain,
stand out in bold relief. The views into Tennessee
and North Carolina extend to the horizon. To
your east, the prominent peak with the imposing
name of Thunderhead competes with the sky.
Take in the view from this rock outcrop just as
others have done for generations.

> **DIRECTIONS**: From the park entrance at Townsend,
> Tennessee, head forward to the Townsend "Wye." Turn
> right here onto Laurel Creek Road, and follow it for 5.6
> miles southwest towards Cades Cove. The Lead Cove Trail
> is on your left, just beyond a small parking area that
> extends on both sides of the road.

Buckhorn Gap *via Meigs Creek*

SCENERY: ✿ ✿ ✿ ✿
DIFFICULTY: ✿ ✿
TRAIL CONDITIONS: ✿ ✿ ✿
SOLITUDE: ✿ ✿ ✿ ✿ ✿
CHILDREN: ✿ ✿ ✿
DISTANCE: *6.8 miles round-trip*
HIKING TIME: *3:00 round-trip*
OUTSTANDING FEATURES: *Meigs Creek valley*

ONCE YOU LEAVE THE CROWDS *at The Sinks behind, you'll
probably have this intimate slice of the Smokies to yourself. This trail
allows you to notice the smaller subtle features of a Southern
Appalachian mountain valley. Meigs Creek will surely catch your eye,
as you cross it nearly 20 times. Not to worry, though, as most crossings are not difficult in times of normal water flow.*

🚶 Once on the Meigs Creek Trail, swing past
The Sinks, a popular swimming and sunbathing
spot. Immediately drop into a boggy area,
unusual for the Smokies, that was once part of
the Little River. Begin ascending onto a dry,
piny ridge and notice the change in forest from
the Little River valley. Wind back down and
finally encounter the trail's namesake, Meigs
Creek, at mile 1.0.

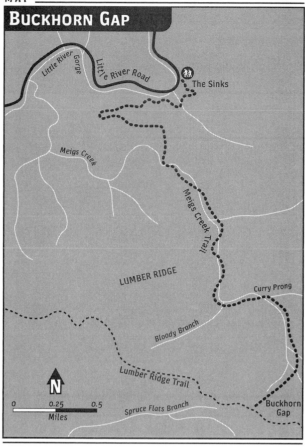

BUCKHORN GAP

Little River Gorge

Little River Road

The Sinks

Meigs Creek

Meigs Creek Trail

LUMBER RIDGE

Curry Prong

Bloody Branch

N

0   0.25   0.5
Miles

Lumber Ridge Trail

Spruce Flats Branch

Buckhorn Gap

The crossings begin here as the creek and trail merge amid a dark green forest interspersed with crashing cascades that flow beneath thickets of rhododendron. After the fourth crossing, a particularly comely falls announces its presence on your right. Continue fording, but stop to notice the clarity of the stream. The people who settled these coves revered their Smoky Mountain water and couldn't get used to drinking "still" well water after they left their highland homes.

As you continue to climb slightly, Meigs Creek and the side creeks that feed it become smaller. Toward the head of the valley, you'll notice that loggers left certain large hemlock trees behind. They were not considered commercially

BUCKHORN GAP

Buckhorn
Gap

Meigs
Creek

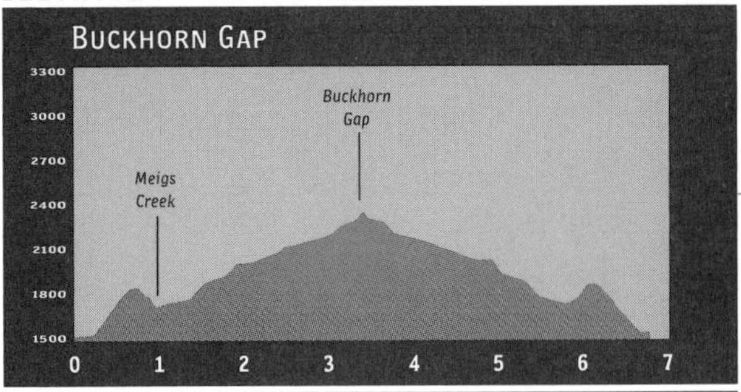

valuable in the early twentieth century and were
left to become the giants of the forest they are
today. The final climb at mile 3.3 signals your
impending arrival at Buckhorn Gap, at mile 3.4.
You'll intersect the Meigs Mountain Trail, which
goes to Elkmont, and the Lumber Ridge Trail,
which goes to Tremont.

> DIRECTIONS: From the Sugarlands Visitor Center,
> drive 12 miles east on the Little River Road to The Sinks
> parking area, on your left. The Meigs Creek Trail starts at
> the rear of the parking area.

Blanket Mountain *via Jakes Creek*

SCENERY: ✰ ✰ ✰ ✰
DIFFICULTY: ✰ ✰
TRAIL CONDITIONS: ✰ ✰ ✰ ✰
SOLITUDE: ✰ ✰ ✰ ✰
CHILDREN: ✰ ✰ ✰
DISTANCE: *8 miles round-trip*
HIKING TIME: *4:00 round-trip*
OUTSTANDING FEATURES: *limited views from Blanket Mountain, ideal
picnic spot*

THIS HIKE STARTS ALONG *noisy Jakes Creek and ends atop
Blanket Mountain, site of a former fire tower. Despite forest
encroachment, an open glade still persists on top of the mountain and
makes an ideal spot for a 4,600-foot-high country picnic on top of
old Smoky. Follow a railroad grade most of your journey in this
watershed of bygone logging and human settlement.*

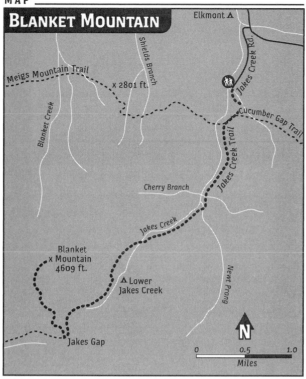

BLANKET MOUNTAIN

Elkmont ▲

Shields Branch

Meigs Mountain Trail

x 2801 ft.

Blanket Creek

Jakes Creek Rd.

Cucumber Gap Trail

Jakes Creek Trail

Cherry Branch

Jakes Creek

Blanket
x Mountain
4609 ft.

▲ Lower
Jakes Creek

Newt Prong

Jakes Gap

N

0   0.5   1.0
Miles

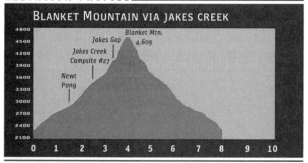

BLANKET MOUNTAIN VIA JAKES CREEK

Blanket Mtn.
Jakes Gap   4,609
Jakes Creek
Campsite #27

Newt
Pong

4800
4500
4200
3900
3600
3300
3000
2700
2400
2100

0 1 2 3 4 5 6 7 8 9 10

🥾 The park's last permanent lifetime resident, Lem Ownby, lived not far from the trailhead. He passed away in 1980, at the age of 91. When the park was formed, many residents deeded over their lands, then were given lifetime leases that allowed them to live out their days in the mountains they cherished.

The Jakes Creek Trail leaves the end of Jakes Creek Road, winding upward to meet the Cucumber Gap Trail at mile 0.3. Continue forward on the jeep road and pass through the Meigs Mountain Trail junction at mile 0.4. The trail begins rising a bit more steadily, crossing Waterdog Branch, then Newt Prong at mile 1.5. The trail narrows as you leave reforested cropland to switchback to the left, then again parallels Jakes Creek below.

After crossing a couple of side branches, you come to Jakes Creek Backcountry Campsite #27, at mile 2.5. Continue working your way to the head of the watershed until you reach Jakes Gap and a trail intersection at mile 3.3. To your left, the Miry Ridge Trail goes 4.9 miles to the Appalachian Trail. Turn right and trace the Blanket Mountain Trail, which is less maintained but still used.

As the trail winds its way up to the summit of Blanket Mountain, where a surveyor once hung a blanket as a marker to delineate Indian lands, you pass a rock outcrop on your left. Step atop the rocks and peer westward across nearby park land. Just beyond the outcrop, at mile 4.0, come to the summit of Blanket Mountain. The remains of the fire tower and cabin make a good table and backrest for the weary and hungry hiker. Blanket Mountain is an idyllic place to laze away a summer's day, escaping the heat of the lowlands.

part one OUT AND BACK

DIRECTIONS: From the Sugarlands Visitor Center, drive 4.9 miles on Little River Road to Elkmont. Turn left and follow the road 1.3 miles till you reach the Elkmont campground. Turn left at a sign for the Little River and Jakes Creek trailheads. Drive 0.5 mile, then follow the right fork 0.5 mile farther to the end at the parking area. Jakes Creek Trail starts from the rear of the parking area and to the left as you enter.

Silers Bald

THIS HIKE FAIRLY EXUDES THE AURA *of the high country, as you traverse in and out of the spruce-fir forest that cloaks only the highest mantles of this land. Straddle the very spine of the state-line ridge, which offers windswept vistas into both Tennessee and North Carolina. Once you've reached the top of Silers Bald, you can look back and see where you started—Clingmans Dome parking area.*

🚶🚶 Start your hike on the Forney Ridge Trail, leaving from the Clingmans Dome parking area. At mile 0.1 veer right on the Clingmans Dome Bypass Trail. After a moderate climb to mile 0.6, you'll intersect the Appalachian Trail near Mount Buckley (elevation 6,500 feet). Continue west on the A.T., descending through an old burned-over section with views. Drop into a saddle, then briefly ascend to a rock outcrop that makes a wonderful bench. Sit awhile and look far into North Carolina.

Enter the spruce-fir forest again, moving downward all the while. It is nearly always wet and cool here, pungent with the aroma of rich earth and growing and decaying vegetation. After a brief level section, come to the Goshen Prong Trail junction at mile 2.7. Continue your descent on the A.T. to arrive at the Double Springs Gap Trail shelter at mile 3.1. A small clearing is in front of the shelter. As you arrive at the shelter, the spring to your left, in North Carolina, is the easiest place to obtain water.

Leave the shelter behind and climb atop Jenkins Knob, jumbled with beech trees. Beech leaves turn brown and often stay on the tree throughout the winter, rattling in the wind.

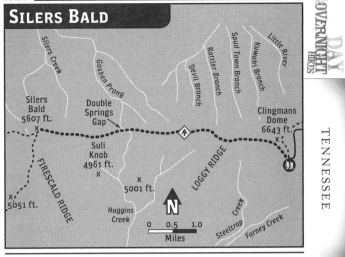

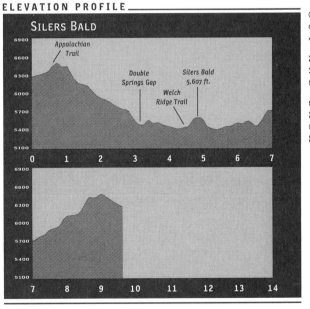

Below the knob you'll come to a field at mile 3.5.
Welch Ridge lines the horizon to your right as
you look into North Carolina. Pass through The
Narrows, where the state-line ridge is barely wide
enough for a footpath.

The Welch Ridge Trail junction intersects the
A.T. at mile 4.4. Begin the final push to arrive
on top of Silers Bald (elevation 5,607 feet) at

mile 4.8. Look back at the rugged crest of the Smokies. As you arrive at Silers Bald, a small side trail to your right allows long views into Tennessee. The A.T. continues down the shrinking bald to your left, which the park service is allowing to become reforested. Relax in what remains of the field and take it all in.

DIRECTIONS: From Newfound Gap, drive 7 miles to the end of Clingmans Dome Road. The Forney Ridge Trail starts at the tip of the Clingmans Dome parking area.

Injun Creek *from Greenbrier*

SCENERY: ✿ ✿ ✿ ✿
DIFFICULTY: ✿
TRAIL CONDITIONS: ✿ ✿ ✿ ✿
SOLITUDE: ✿ ✿ ✿ ✿ ✿
CHILDREN: ✿ ✿ ✿ ✿
DISTANCE: *6.4 miles round-trip*
HIKING TIME: *3:30 round-trip*
OUTSTANDING FEATURES: *old homesites, small creeks, old steam engine*

TAKE A WALK THROUGH TIME *on this hike, which skirts the lower reaches of Mount LeConte, passing a collection of former farms and homesites that dot the Greenbrier area. The hike culminates at Injun Creek Backcountry Campsite, above which lies an old steam engine, a relic of the settler days in the Smokies. This isolated, historic walk is one of the most underrated and underused in the park.*

🚶 Your hike starts on the Grapeyard Ridge Trail, which follows an old road used by area settlers. You'll pass rock walls and more old roads that splinter off the trail. Ascend a small ridge and, at mile 0.6, you'll find an old homesite and the remains of a chimney. The trail follows a small brook leading to Rhododendron Creek. As you enter an old field, you will begin the first of several crossings of Rhododendron Creek and its tributaries, none of which are deep, though you may wet your boots a bit.

Wind up the creek valley, noting homesites on both sides of the trail. The 1931 topographic map of the Smokies shows 11 homesites in the

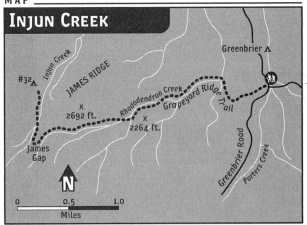

INJUN CREEK

Greenbrier ▲

#32 ▲

Injun Creek

JAMES RIDGE

X 2692 ft.

Rhododendron Creek

Grapeyard Ridge Trail

X 2264 ft.

James Gap

Greenbrier Road

Porters Creek

N

| 0 | 0.5 | 1.0 |

Miles

DAY & OVERNIGHT HIKES

TENNESSEE

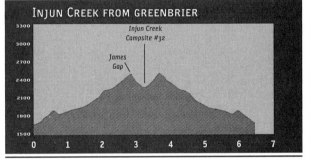

INJUN CREEK FROM GREENBRIER

Injun Creek Campsite #32

James Gap

part one
OUT AND BACK

Rhododendron Creek watershed. Rhododendron, the creek's namesake, constrict the path in
areas near the creek, but the trail opens up away
from water.

At mile 2.2, leave Rhododendron Creek and
begin the ascent to James Gap. Another homesite
sits in the saddle of James Gap at mile 2.8. Enter
the Injun Creek watershed. As you descend, the
inspiration for the name Injun Creek appears in
a rivulet on your right. The body and wheels of a
tractor-like steam engine lie upturned, water
running beneath the engine's rusted hulk. Some-
where in the naming of this creek, an errant
mapmaker thought the name Injun Creek
referred to Indians rather than this old steam
"enjun" that made its final turn in the Smoky
Mountains.

The road-turned-trail descends to reach the side trail to Injun Creek Backcountry Campsite #32. Turn right on the side trail to the camp at mile 3.2, where there is yet another homesite. Walk around and look at the lasting changes the settlers made on the land, such as creating level ground with rock-wall terraces. The campsite makes for a good break spot. On your return journey, try to visualize how this area will look once the forest reestablishes itself over this part of the Smokies.

> DIRECTIONS: From Gatlinburg, drive 6 miles east on US 321 to Greenbrier. Turn right at the Greenbrier sign and follow Greenbrier Road 3.1 miles to the intersection with Ramsey Prong Road, which crosses a bridge to your left. Park just before the intersection. The Grapeyard Ridge Trail starts on the right side of Greenbrier Road.

Albright Grove

SCENERY: ✿ ✿ ✿ ✿	
DIFFICULTY: ✿ ✿	
TRAIL CONDITIONS: ✿ ✿ ✿ ✿ ✿	
SOLITUDE: ✿ ✿ ✿	
CHILDREN: ✿ ✿ ✿	
DISTANCE: 6.8 miles round-trip	
HIKING TIME: 3:15 round-trip	
OUTSTANDING FEATURES: huge old-growth forest, pioneer cabin	

A HARD-TO-FIND TRAILHEAD *keeps a lot of hikers off this trail. However, with good directions, it's a cinch. From the starting point, head up a wide bed on the Maddron Bald Trail, passing the Willis Baxter cabin, still intact after more than a century. Pass through a trail junction and start to climb a bit, then come to the side trail leading into Albright Grove. This nature trail loops through a giant forest of hemlock and tulip trees, located between Dunn and Indian Camp creeks. The immensity of this woodland, named after former National Park Service Director Horace Albright, lures you to repeat the trek with friends in tow.*

🚶 Pass around a pole gate and a trail sign. Head up an open trailbed beneath a second-growth deciduous forest that was once farmland. Remember the size of these trees, so you can

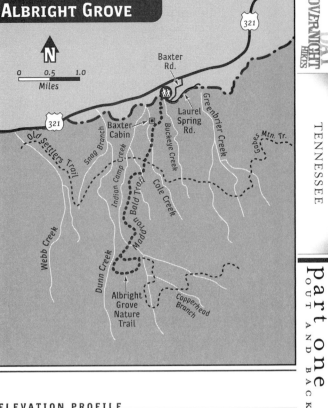

ALBRIGHT GROVE

N

0   0.5   1.0
Miles

321

Baxter
Rd.

Baxter Branch

Laurel Spring Rd.

Greenbrier Creek

Gabes Mtn. Tr.

321

Old Settlers Trail

Snag Branch

Baxter Cabin

Indian Camp Creek

Buckeye Creek

Cole Creek

Bald Trail

Maddron

Webb Creek

Dunn Creek

Albright Grove Nature Trail

Copperhead Branch

ELEVATION PROFILE

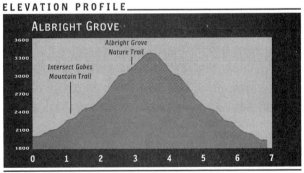

ALBRIGHT GROVE

Albright Grove
Nature Trail

Intersect Gabes
Mountain Trail

3600
3300
3000
2700
2400
2100
1800

0   1   2   3   4   5   6   7

compare them with their larger cousins up the
path. The trail levels off and comes to the Willis
Baxter cabin at 0.5 mile. This one-room cabin
was built in 1889. Observe the notched logs at the
corners of the cabin. Nearby you will find rock
walls and a small, rocked-in spring. Developed
springs are almost always found near old pioneer

cabins and homesites, because reliable water sources often lured homesteaders.

Keep up the Maddron Bald Trail, coming to a trail junction at mile 1.2. The Gabes Mountain Trail leaves left and the Old Settlers Trail departs right. History buffs can make a little side trip down the Old Settlers Trail to see more homesites. Tree enthusiasts should continue on the Maddron Bald Trail, which narrows and steepens a bit. Parallel Indian Camp Creek, and come to an old auto turnaround at mile 2.3. The path narrows yet again. Soon, cross Indian Camp Creek and reach the Albright Grove Nature Trail at mile 2.9. Turn right here and revel in the land of the giants. Some of the grove's largest tulip trees have massive circumferences. There are other species here, such as Fraser magnolia, beech, and Carolina silverbell. Reach the end of the nature trail at mile 3.7. Turn back down the Maddron Bald Trail. Your return trip will be 3.1 miles long.

DIRECTIONS: Take US 321, East Parkway, north from Gatlinburg for 15.6 miles to Baxter Road. (Baxter Road is just beyond Jellystone Park Campground and Smoky Mountain Creekside Rentals.) Turn right onto Baxter Road and follow it for 0.3 mile to the gravel Laurel Springs Road. Veer sharply right onto Laurel Springs Road and follow it for 100 yards to a pole gate and trail sign on the left. The Maddron Bald Trail starts here.

Sutton Ridge Overlook

SCENERY: ✩ ✩ ✩ ✩
DIFFICULTY: ✩ ✩
TRAIL CONDITIONS: ✩ ✩ ✩ ✩ ✩
SOLITUDE: ✩ ✩ ✩ ✩
CHILDREN: ✩ ✩ ✩ ✩
DISTANCE: *3.0 miles round-trip*
HIKING TIME: *1:45 round-trip*
OUTSTANDING FEATURES: *views, pioneer history*

THIS IS A MODERATE HIKE *to a great view. It's a wonder its not hiked more. The walk starts near Cosby Campground and passes through former pioneer lands, long since reforested. Cross a brook-*

SUTTON RIDGE OVERLOOK

Camel Gap Trail

Snake Den Trail

Gabes Mountain Trail

GABES MOUNTAIN

32

Cosby Campground

Cosby Creek

SUTTON RIDGE

Low Gap Trail

Overlook

Toms Creek

Riding Fork

Gilliand Creek

Mount Cammerer Tower

Lower Mount Cammerer Trail

32

N

0   0.5   1
Mile

ELEVATION PROFILE

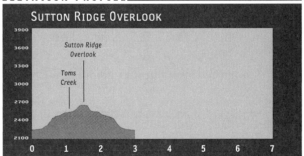

SUTTON RIDGE OVERLOOK

3900
3600   Sutton Ridge Overlook
3300
3000   Toms Creek
2700
2400
2100
0   1   2   3   4   5   6   7

---

trout stream while looking for signs of settlement, then climb a bit to Sutton Ridge. Take the side trail to a great view of the surrounding area. This hike is ideal for families that want to get off the beaten path, or for anyone who just wants a rewarding leg stretcher.

🚶 Leave the Cosby hiker parking area and take the Low Gap Trail. Cosby Creek lies to your left. Cruise through a forest of maple, buckeye, and hemlock. Pass the Cosby campground amphitheater and keep forward as the Cosby Nature Trail forks left. Look for crumbled bits of pavement on this old road. Pass over small streams on a series of footbridges. The Cosby Nature Trail now comes in from the left. The Low Gap Trail continues forward to a trail junction in a flat at 0.4 mile.

Turn left and follow the Low Gap Trail just a few more steps to the beginning of the Lower Mount Cammerer Trail. Keep forward on the latter, as the Low Gap Trail forks right. Begin to look for evidence of settlers, such as rock walls and an old rocked-in spring. Tulip trees grow overhead. They like to invade former fields. At mile 1.1, come to Toms Creek. This stream is a brook-trout habitat. Brook trout are the only native Smokies trout and are normally relegated to higher-elevation streams, due to heavy stocking in the past of rainbow and brown trout. But Toms Creek, at 2,500 feet, still sports brookies.

After crossing Toms Creek on a footbridge, begin the short ascent to Sutton Ridge, reached at 1.4 miles. There is a horse hitch here. Turn right on the marked overlook trail and follow it 200 yards through woods of pine and oak to a clearing. Here, a splendid vista rewards hikers. To your left is the upper Cosby Valley. Gabes Mountain is the prominent mountain to your left. Ahead is lower Cosby Valley, and to your right is Gililand Ridge on lower Mount Cammerer.

DIRECTIONS: From Gatlinburg, take US 321 north until it comes to a T intersection with TN 32. Turn right on TN 32 and follow it a little over a mile to the signed right turn into the Cosby section of the park. At 2.1 miles on Cosby Road, turn left into the hiker parking area. The Low Gap Trail starts at the upper end of the parking area.

Brushy Mountain

SCENERY: ✿ ✿ ✿ ✿ ✿
DIFFICULTY: ✿ ✿ ✿
TRAIL CONDITIONS: ✿ ✿ ✿ ✿
SOLITUDE: ✿ ✿ ✿ ✿
CHILDREN: ✿ ✿
DISTANCE: *11.4 miles round-trip*
HIKING TIME: *5:30 round-trip*
OUTSTANDING FEATURES: *old homesites, views from atop Brushy Mountain*

THIS HIKE PASSES THROUGH OLD FARMING AREAS, *ascends through dry ridge country and a hemlock forest, and arrives at Trillium Gap. A short climb leads you to the top of Brushy Mountain, where views await amid a heath-bald plant community. The more than 2,500-foot climb is steady, but the varied forest types and the view at the end are well worth the effort.*

🚶 Leave Greenbrier Road on the Porters Creek Trail. The crashing Porters Creek will be your companion as you gently rise, passing the Ownby Cemetery about a half-mile from the trailhead. The Brushy Mountain Trail junction is reached at mile 1.0. Follow Brushy Mountain Trail as it leaves the junction at the far end of a loop and enters an old farm community located in Porters Flat. Old rock walls, chimneys, and discarded metal items are all that remain of lives led in the shadow of nearby Mount LeConte.

At mile 2.2, a small side trail leads down on your right to Fittified Spring, whose name is a first-rate example of mountain-folk vernacular (the spring has apparently steadied its flow nowadays). The trail passes near Long Branch but veers back south while leaving Porters Flat behind. The climb to Brushy Mountain remains steady as the trail enters a pine-oak forest, prevalent on south-facing slopes.

At mile 3.1, a large boulder to your right offers a nice combination vista and rest spot. Continue climbing and cross Trillium Branch twice, into a forest now dominated by hemlock trees. At mile 5.5, you'll reach grassy Trillium

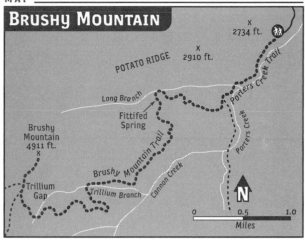

BRUSHY MOUNTAIN

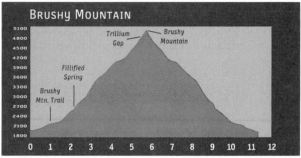

Gap. This is one of those mountain places with a perpetual cool breeze, demanding hikers stop to absorb the ambiance beneath the beech trees.

To reach the top of Brushy Mountain, veer right from the gap and follow the path beneath the tunnel of rhododendron and mountain laurel, which are the primary components of the heath—bald community. Come to an opening in the bald at mile 5.7. Brushy Mountain offers panoramas both above and below your 4,900-foot elevation. Above and to your south is the imposing bulk of Mount LeConte. To your east lies Porters Creek valley where you started. Below, to the north, are Gatlinburg and East Tennessee.

Ramsay Cascade

SCENERY: ✿ ✿ ✿ ✿ ✿
DIFFICULTY: ✿ ✿ ✿
TRAIL CONDITIONS: ✿ ✿ ✿
SOLITUDE: ✿ ✿
CHILDREN: ✿ ✿ ✿
DISTANCE: *8.0 miles round-trip*
HIKING TIME: *4:00 round-trip*
OUTSTANDING FEATURES: *old-growth forest, falls at end of trail*

THIS IS A POPULAR ROUTE *with well-deserved rewards, not only at the end, but also during the hike itself. It starts out with a slight upgrade, then climbs more steeply as it nears the falls. The steeper portion of the trail is lined with old-growth trees that never saw the logger's axe, or any settlement for that matter. The area remains as it has for ages.*

🚶🚶 Start your hike on the Ramsay Cascade Trail, on the south side of the Middle Prong of the Little Pigeon River. Cross over the prong on a very long footbridge, and wind your way past Ramsay Branch, which flows from Greenbrier Pinnacle, the formation on the left that shades the trail. At mile 1.5, the trail comes to a turnaround. The Greenbrier Pinnacle Trail, no longer maintained, splits off to the left. The Ramsay Cascade Trail continues forward and begins to climb more steeply.

Cross back to the south side of Ramsay Prong on a footlog at mile 3.1, then climb away from the main creek to cross and recross a small branch, continually gaining elevation. This is the valley of the big trees: tulip, Carolina silverbells, and eastern hemlocks, among others. Traverse Ramsay Prong yet again on another footlog as you near the cascades, at mile 3.7. Exposed roots on the hiker-worn path can make the trail tricky, especially while you're looking around at all the big trees.

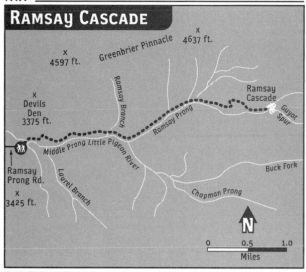

RAMSAY CASCADE

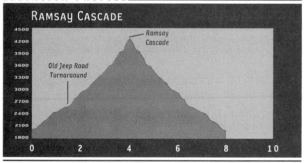

Plunging down the green valley, between the high ridges of Guyot Spur and Pinnacle Lead, is Ramsay Cascade (elevation 4,300 feet), at mile 4.0. Though it falls less than 100 feet, the cascade sends out quite a spray. Picnickers and trail-weary hikers always seem to find a great view from a suitable rock to watch this natural water show.

DIRECTIONS: From Gatlinburg, drive 6 miles east on US 321 to Greenbrier. Turn right at the Greenbrier sign and follow Greenbrier Road 3.1 miles to the intersection with Ramsay Prong Road, which crosses a bridge to your left. Turn left on Ramsay Prong Road and follow it for 1.5 miles to the parking area at the end of the road. The Ramsay Cascade Trail starts at the rear of the parking area.

Mount Cammerer *via Low Gap*

> SCENERY: ✿ ✿ ✿ ✿ ✿
> DIFFICULTY: ✿ ✿ ✿
> TRAIL CONDITIONS: ✿ ✿ ✿
> SOLITUDE: ✿ ✿ ✿ ✿
> CHILDREN: ✿ ✿
> DISTANCE: *10.8 miles round-trip*
> HIKING TIME: *5:15 round-trip*
> OUTSTANDING FEATURES: *historic fire tower, views from atop*
> *Mount Cammerer*

FORMERLY CALLED WHITE ROCK *by Tennesseans and Sharp Top by Carolinians, this mountaintop rock outcrop was renamed by the park service after Arno B. Cammerer, a former director of the National Park Service. No matter the name, this peak has incredible panoramas from its place on the Smokies crest. A historic wood and stone fire tower, long in disuse, has been repaired by a group known as Friends of the Smokies. The restoration makes Mount Cammerer an even more desirable destination.*

🚶 The trek to Cammerer starts in Cosby at the hiker parking area on the Low Gap Trail. Follow the newer path, which skirts the campground for 0.3 mile to the old Low Gap Trail, once maintained as a road to the fire tower. Enter farmland-turned-woodland to cross Cosby Creek on a footbridge at mile 0.9.

The trail begins a steady but not too steep climb toward the Smokies crest. The wide roadbed allows you to look around without having to watch your every step. At mile 1.3, the trail makes the first of several switchbacks amid a nearly virgin forest. Cross Cosby Creek (now tiny) again at mile 2.5, as the trail works its way toward Low Gap, where it meets the Appalachian Trail at mile 2.9.

At Low Gap, turn left on the A.T. and resume your ascent. This section of the A.T. is much less used than the section near Newfound Gap. After a mile of steady climbing, the A.T. levels out near Sunup Knob, at mile 3.9. The trail is as level as trails come in the Smokies, rising slightly near the junction with the Mount Cammerer Trail at mile 4.9.

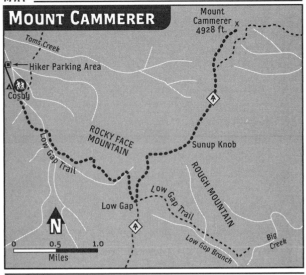

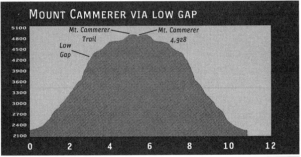

Turn left on the Mount Cammerer Trail and follow the spur ridge out of the wooded junction into an area dominated by mountain laurel. After a slight dip, you'll reach the outcrop and tower at mile 5.4. Though it does enhance the setting, you don't need to climb the restored tower to enjoy the vistas from the jutting rocks, for you can see in every direction from the outcrop. The rock cut of Interstate 40 is visible to your east. Mount Sterling and its fire tower are to your south. In the foreground to the north is the appropriately named Stone Mountain. Beyond Stone Mountain, to the horizon's end, lies Tennessee. Maybe a place this spectacular does deserve three names.

> DIRECTIONS: From Gatlinburg, take US 321 east until
> it comes to a T intersection with TN 32. Turn right on TN
> 32 and follow it a little over a mile, turning right into the
> signed Cosby section of the park. At 2.1 miles, come to the
> hiker parking area to the left of the campground registra-
> tion hut. The Low Gap Trail starts in the upper corner of
> the parking area.

Andrews Bald

SCENERY: ✿ ✿ ✿ ✿ ✿
DIFFICULTY: ✿
TRAIL CONDITIONS: ✿ ✿ ✿ ✿
SOLITUDE: ✿ ✿
CHILDREN: ✿ ✿ ✿ ✿ ✿
DISTANCE: *3.6 miles round-trip*
HIKING TIME: *1:45 round-trip*
OUTSTANDING FEATURES: *spruce-fir forest, Andrews Bald*

THIS IS ONE OF THE SMOKIES' FINEST HIKES. *The trip
passes through an extraordinary spruce-fir forest to the grassy field of
Andrews Bald. Resplendent with stunning views, this is an ideal backdrop for a picnic in the sky. Andrews Bald is one of only two grassy
fields in the Smokies that the park service maintains in their "original"
state. The origin of these fields is not clear, although fire, Indians, and
cattle are thought to be possibilities.*

🏃 After leaving the Clingmans Dome parking area
on the Forney Ridge Trail, you zigzag through an
evergreen forest reminiscent of Maine or Canada.
At 0.1 mile into the hike, make sure you veer left,
away from the Clingmans Dome Bypass Trail. The
Forney Ridge Trail descends along a rocky section
that allows views southward and, at mile 1.0, intersects the Forney Creek Trail.

Continue forward along the undulating and
rocky ridge to arrive at the southern end of
Andrews Bald at mile 1.8. The lush grassy field
(elevation 5,800 feet) beckons you to lie down,
but that would deny you the expansive views of the
southern range of the Smokies and beyond, as far
south as the clarity of the sky allows. This bald,
the Smokies' highest, also offers marvelous flower
displays in June, as well as blueberries and black-
berries in late summer.

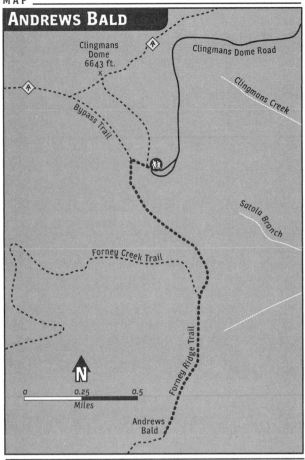

ANDREWS BALD

Clingmans Dome 6643 ft.
x

Clingmans Dome Road

Clingmans Creek

Bypass Trail

Satola Branch

Forney Creek Trail

Forney Ridge Trail

N

| 0 | 0.25 | 0.5 |

Miles

Andrews Bald

ELEVATION PROFILE

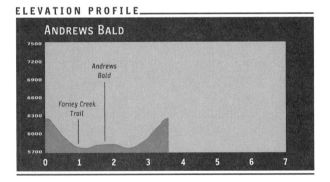

ANDREWS BALD

7500		
7200	Andrews Bald	
6900		
6600		
6300	Forney Creek Trail	
6000		
5700		

0   1   2   3   4   5   6   7

DIRECTIONS: From Newfound Gap, drive 7 miles to the end of Clingmans Dome Road. The Forney Ridge Trail starts at the tip of the Clingmans Dome parking area.

Mount Sterling
via Mount Sterling Gap

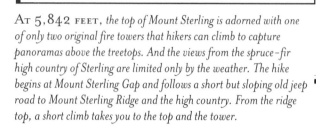

SCENERY: ✿ ✿ ✿ ✿ ✿

DIFFICULTY: ✿ ✿

TRAIL CONDITIONS: ✿ ✿ ✿ ✿ ✿

SOLITUDE: ✿ ✿ ✿ ✿

CHILDREN: ✿ ✿ ✿

DISTANCE: *5.6 miles round-trip*

HIKING TIME: *2:45 round-trip*

OUTSTANDING FEATURES: *excellent views from Mount Sterling tower*

AT 5,842 FEET, *the top of Mount Sterling is adorned with one of only two original fire towers that hikers can climb to capture panoramas above the treetops. And the views from the spruce-fir high country of Sterling are limited only by the weather. The hike begins at Mount Sterling Gap and follows a short but sloping old jeep road to Mount Sterling Ridge and the high country. From the ridge top, a short climb takes you to the top and the tower.*

🚶 Leave Mount Sterling Gap (elevation 3,890 feet) and begin climbing steeply up the wooded mountainside. The trail levels out a bit as it comes to an open area and the Long Bunk Trail junction at mile 0.4. Resume climbing and make a sharp switchback to the right at mile 0.7.

The climb doesn't slacken much as it switchbacks further up the mountain until it reaches the Mount Sterling Ridge Trail junction in a small grassy area at mile 2.3. The trail has now climbed 1,600 feet. Turn right at the junction, staying on the Mount Sterling Trail. Hike through forested and grassy areas, then pass a horse-hitch rack just before arriving at the top of Mount Sterling at mile 2.8. The mountaintop is also the location of Mount Sterling Backcountry Campsite #38.

The tower is at the crest of the mountain. Baxter Creek Trail, which comes from the Big Creek Ranger Station, also ends at the tower. If you are thirsty, a spring can be found on a side trail, a half-mile down the Baxter Creek Trail to your left (don't forget to treat the water). The

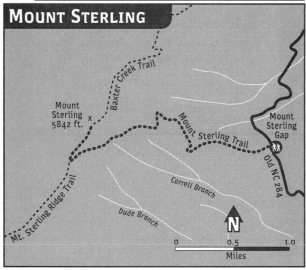

MOUNT STERLING

Baxter Creek Trail

Mount
Sterling
5842 ft.

Mount Sterling Trail

Mount
Sterling
Gap

Old NC 284

Correll Branch

Dude Branch

Mt. Sterling Ridge Trail

N

| 0 | 0.5 | 1.0 |

Miles

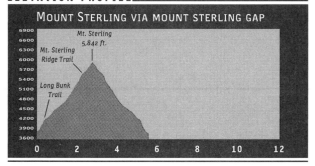

MOUNT STERLING VIA MOUNT STERLING GAP

Mt. Sterling
5,842 ft.

Mt. Sterling
Ridge Trail

Long Bunk
Trail

6900
6600
6300
6000
5700
5400
5100
4800
4500
4200
3900
3600

0   2   4   6   8   10   12

park's eastern edge is the featured view from the
tower. The main crest of the Smokies lies to the
north. To the east, I-40 cuts through the
Pigeon River gorge. In the summer, the grassy
area below the tower is an ideal lunch spot.

DIRECTIONS: From Interstate 40, take exit 451, for
Waterville. Cross the Pigeon River before turning left to
follow it upstream. At an intersection 2.3 miles after
crossing the Pigeon River, turn left on old NC 284 in
Mount Sterling Village. Follow the dirt road 7 miles to
Mount Sterling Gap. The Mount Sterling Trail starts on
your right at the gap.

Flat Creek Falls

SCENERY: ✿ ✿ ✿ ✿ ✿
DIFFICULTY: ✿ ✿
TRAIL CONDITIONS: ✿ ✿ ✿ ✿
SOLITUDE: ✿ ✿ ✿ ✿
CHILDREN: ✿ ✿ ✿ ✿
DISTANCE: *3.2 miles round-trip*
HIKING TIME: *2:00 round-trip*
OUTSTANDING FEATURES: *view, waterfall, attractive high-country woodland*

THIS IS THE SORT OF ROUTE *that makes hikers wonder, "Why aren't more people hiking this trail?" Maybe because the Flat Creek Trail begins on a lesser-traveled road, or maybe because it has no other trail connections. For Smoky Mountain enthusiasts there should be no maybes about hiking this path. It starts at more than 5,300 feet and passes a wonderful view of the Smokies' crest before entering a high-country forest of spruce and yellow birch. The path then descends along Flat Creek and makes its way to the highest elevation falls accessible by trail in the park. Be careful and keep children under control around this steep and narrow cascade. Otherwise, it is a fine family hike.*

🏃 Start the walk on the Flat Creek Trail, swinging around the Heintooga Picnic Area on the left. At 0.1 mile, near a water fountain, come to a cleared overlook. To the north is the crest of the Smokies. With binoculars you can see the Clingmans Dome tower. Keep forward and soon come to a trail junction. Drop down to the right on a narrow path. Overhead are tall spruces and yellow birches. Soon, work your way around the knob that once held Flat Creek Bald. It is forested now, though the understory remains grassy. Reach Flat Creek at 0.7 mile. You easily cross the small stream on a footbridge.

Keep a fairly level course through a pleasant woodland, crossing Flat Creek twice more on footlogs, just beyond mile 1.0. Wet-weather drainages bisect the trailbed from the left as the trail moves away from the creek. Reach the side trail for Flat Creek Falls at mile 1.5. Turn right here and descend toward Flat Creek. The sound

FLAT CREEK FALLS

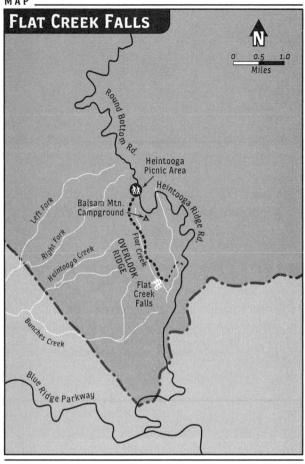

of rushing water becomes audible as you near Flat Creek, at mile 1.6. Keep kids under close supervision in this area, as Flat Creek puts gravity to use on its way to meet Bunches Creek in the valley below. There are views of the Bunches Creek watershed near Flat Creek. Side trails spur down toward the steep, narrow fall. It is challenging to get a complete view of the entire cascade, as the fall is narrow and drops down a heavily vegetated rock chute. Nevertheless, stunning glimpses abound, rewarding hikers for their trek.

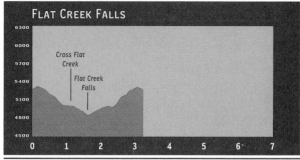

FLAT CREEK FALLS

Cross Flat
Creek

Flat Creek
Falls

DIRECTIONS: From the Oconaluftee Visitor Center near Cherokee, take Newfound Gap Road for 0.5 mile south to the Blue Ridge Parkway. Turn left onto the Blue Ridge Parkway and follow it for 10.8 miles to Heintooga Ridge Road. Turn left on Heintooga Ridge Road and go 8.7 miles to the Heintooga Picnic Area. The Flat Creek Falls Trail starts at the end of the auto turnaround near the picnic area.

Little Cataloochee Church

SCENERY: ✪ ✪ ✪ ✪

DIFFICULTY: ✪ ✪

TRAIL CONDITIONS: ✪ ✪ ✪ ✪

SOLITUDE: ✪ ✪ ✪ ✪ ✪

CHILDREN: ✪ ✪ ✪ ✪

DISTANCE: *7.6 miles round-trip*

HIKING TIME: *3:45 round-trip*

OUTSTANDING FEATURES: *multiple historic homesites, Little Cataloochee Church*

THE HIKE TO LITTLE CATALOOCHEE BAPTIST *church traverses an historic mountain valley setting left over from the last century. Starting on Pretty Hollow Gap Trail, you'll hike past old fields and evidence of settlement before turning on the Little Cataloochee Trail. Then you'll climb to Davidson Gap and into the Little Cataloochee valley, with its many old homesites, to finally end up at Little Cataloochee Church. This fine structure was built in 1890 and is maintained to this day.*

🚶 Leave Cataloochee Road and pass the Cataloochee horse camp at mile 0.2. Hike by some old fields, known locally as Indian Flats. They

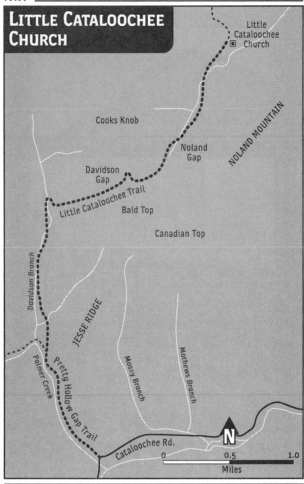

were so named because Indians were there when
the pioneers first set foot in this watershed.
Come to the Little Cataloochee Trail junction at
mile 0.7. Bear right on the Little Cataloochee
Trail, here an old roadbed, heading for Davidson Gap along Davidson Branch, which you'll
cross several times.

Veer right up a tributary of Davidson Branch
at mile 1.7. The trail steepens considerably,
passing the remains of a settler's cabin on the
left before reaching Davidson Gap at mile 2.3.
Descend into the Little Cataloochee Valley,

LITTLE CATALOOCHEE CHURCH

where more settlements were strung along Little Cataloochee Creek and its tributaries.

One tributary, Coggins Branch, will lead you into the valley. Of course, it has homesites of its own, marked by fence posts, rock walls, and old foundations, the most prominent of which is the Dan Cook place at mile 3.0. Built in 1856, the main house is deteriorating in the moist mountain climate, but the stone remnants of the barn are intact.

Pass more reminders of humanity's presence, coming to Little Cataloochee Baptist Church at mile 3.8. After passing so many dilapidated remains, the well-maintained white church looks even more impressive. An accompanying graveyard is nearby. Local families maintain the church.

The church makes a great base for further exploration of the entire valley and its historic settlements. Remember that the remnants are a living archaeological exhibit of life in the Smokies, and artifacts should be left where they are found. Enjoy this hike into history in the Little Cataloochee Valley.

Cabin Flats *via Bradley Fork*

SCENERY: ✩ ✩ ✩ ✩

DIFFICULTY: ✩ ✩

TRAIL CONDITIONS: ✩ ✩ ✩ ✩ ✩

SOLITUDE: ✩ ✩ ✩

CHILDREN: ✩ ✩ ✩ ✩

DISTANCE: *10.4 miles round-trip*

HIKING TIME: *5:15 round-trip*

OUTSTANDING FEATURES: *Bradley Fork, big trees*

THE HIKE TO CABIN FLATS *is a deep-forest venture that shows nature's beauty in countless little ways, as opposed to a hike planned to reach a single vista. The Bradley Fork Trail climbs very gradually on an old jeep road, allowing the hiker to admire Bradley Fork, an archetypal Smoky Mountain stream, as it works its way down to Smokemont amid a forest replete with native flora.*

🚶 On Bradley Fork Trail, leave the Smokemont campground with Bradley Fork on your left. Pass a side road leading to the water supply for Smokemont campground at mile 0.3. Buildings and houses once occupied both sides of Bradley Fork; look for level areas with thin forest cover. Cross a wooden bridge over Chasteen Creek at mile 1.0. Just beyond this crossing is the Chasteen Creek Trail junction. Above this small clearing is Lower Chasteen Creek Backcountry Campsite #50.

Continuing on the Bradley Fork Trail, you come to the Smokemont Loop Trail junction at mile 1.6, then to a horse rail beside a nearby cascade at mile 2.5. The Bradley Fork Trail then crosses an island on Bradley Fork at mile 3.1, by means of two wide bridges. Cross Tabor Branch,

CABIN FLATS

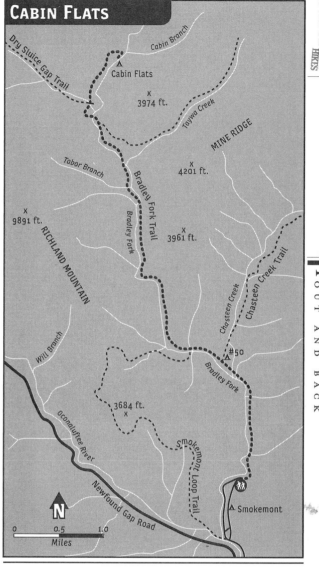

then Bradley Fork again, just as Taywa Creek spills in from the right at mile 3.6.

Follow the jeep road a half-mile farther to the Cabin Flats Trail junction at mile 4.1. Go forward on the Cabin Flats Trail and immediately cross Bradley Fork on an impressive trestle bridge that seems oddly out of place in these old growth

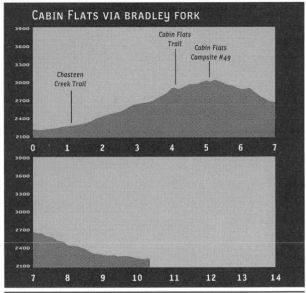

woods. Cross Tennessee Branch on a footbridge, just before the Dry Sluice Gap Trail junction at mile 4.6.

The Cabin Flats Trail winds along the west side of the Bradley Fork valley before descending into Cabin Flats proper, at mile 5.2, after a sharp right turn. This is the location of Cabin Flats Backcountry Campsite #49. The lower end of the campsite offers a nice pool for cooling off. Just below the pool is a massive log jam, a relic of the spring flood of 2003.

DIRECTIONS: From the Oconaluftee Visitor Center, drive 3.2 miles north on Newfound Gap Road. Turn right into the Smokemont campground on a bridge over the Oconaluftee River. Veer left and pass the campground check-in station. The Bradley Fork Trail starts at the gated jeep road at the rear of the campground, on the right as you enter.

Kephart Shelter

via Kephart Prong

SCENERY: ☆ ☆ ☆ ☆

DIFFICULTY: ☆

TRAIL CONDITIONS: ☆ ☆ ☆ ☆ ☆

SOLITUDE: ☆ ☆ ☆

CHILDREN: ☆ ☆ ☆ ☆ ☆

DISTANCE: *4.0 miles round-trip*

HIKING TIME: *2:00 round-trip*

OUTSTANDING FEATURES: *mountain stream, old Civilian Conservation Corps camp*

THIS HIKE EXEMPLIFIES *the effects people have had on the Smokies, and the truly amazing powers nature has to recuperate from such influence. After crossing the Oconaluftee River, you'll enter a former Civilian Conservation Corps (CCC) camp, a relic of the New Deal era of the 1930s. Next is the site of an early park service fish hatchery. Follow the course of Kephart Prong to a backcountry shelter in an old lumber camp. The dry shelter that awaits at journey's end could make this a favorable rainy day hike.*

🏃 Start the hike by crossing the Oconaluftee River on a wide bridge. At mile 0.2, enter the former CCC camp. Pieces of paving, a large chimney, building foundations, scattered tools, and even an old water fountain remain in the second-growth woodland. Explore the area and see what other signs you can spot of the lives of the young men who toiled here.

Veer left beyond the camp and cross Kephart Prong on a footlog at mile 0.3. This footlog, like many others in the park, has a thin veneer of moss and can be slippery in the damp climate of the Smokies. Turn right and trace Kephart Prong. Up ahead is the former fish hatchery. Look around for signs of park employees' efforts to amend the ravages of negligent logging before birth of the Smoky Mountains National Park. For example, logging silted streams and killed fish native to the Smokies; hence the fish hatchery.

KEPHART SHELTER

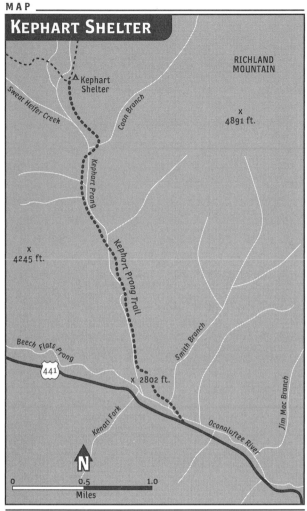

RICHLAND MOUNTAIN

△ Kephart Shelter

Sweat Heifer Creek

Coon Branch

x 4891 ft.

Kephart Prong

Kephart Prong Trail

x 4245 ft.

Beech Flats Prong

Smith Branch

441

x 2802 ft.

Kenati Fork

Oconaluftee River

Jim Mac Branch

N

0   0.5   1.0
Miles

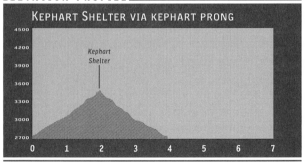

KEPHART SHELTER VIA KEPHART PRONG

Kephart
Shelter

4500
4200
3900
3600
3300
3000
2700

0   1   2   3   4   5   6   7

Cross Kephart Prong on a footlog at mile 0.7 and again at mile 1.0. Be careful to watch for the footlog crossings: they may be up or downstream of where the trail crosses the creek. Kephart Prong Trail is a horse and hiking trail, and horses, of course, do not use the footbridges but wade directly across the creek.

Rejoin the railroad grade, then cross the stream on a fourth footlog at mile 1.5. Continue on the right side of Kephart Prong to arrive at the Kephart shelter at mile 2.0. The stream and shelter, like nearby Mount Kephart, are named for the famed outdoor writer and national park supporter, Horace Kephart. The woods in the Kephart Prong watershed are recovering admirably from the tree harvest of the early 1900s, considering the fact that a logging camp once stood on the site of the shelter. Horace Kephart would be proud of his namesake.

DIRECTIONS: From the Sugarlands Visitors Center, drive south 8.8 miles beyond Newfound Gap on Newfound Gap Road. The Kephart Prong Trail is on your left. From the Oconaluftee Visitor Center, drive 6.8 miles north on Newfound Gap Road. The Kephart Prong Trail is on your right.

Shuckstack
from Twentymile Ranger Station

SCENERY: ☆ ☆ ☆ ☆ ☆
DIFFICULTY: ☆ ☆ ☆
TRAIL CONDITIONS: ☆ ☆ ☆ ☆ ☆
SOLITUDE: ☆ ☆ ☆ ☆
CHILDREN: ☆ ☆
DISTANCE: *10.2 miles round-trip*
HIKING TIME: *5:15 round-trip*
OUTSTANDING FEATURES: *waterfall, views from Shuckstack Mountain*

TWENTYMILE IS ONE OF THE SMOKIES' *most remote areas. You'll travel along Twentymile Creek on an old railroad grade, past Twentymile Cascades, up to the Appalachian Trail and Shuckstack*

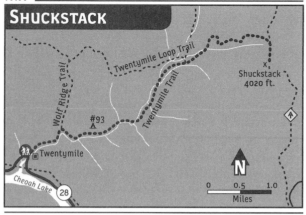

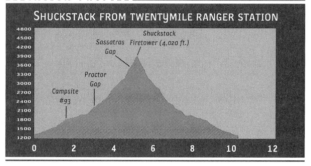

Mountain, and finally to a fire tower that offers one of those worth-the-effort, above-the-treetops, 360-degree panoramas.

Begin your hike at the gated road on the Twentymile Trail. Pass a park service barn in a clearing on your right. Cross Moore Spring Branch on a wide bridge at mile 0.6. On the far side of the bridge is the Wolf Ridge Trail junction. Bear right, staying on the Twentymile Trail. At mile 0.7, a sign marks the side trail to the bottom of Twentymile Cascades. Take the side trail for a view of the creek dropping over a series of wide stone slabs.

Return to the main trail, ascending gradually. Cross Twentymile Creek on wide bridges at miles 1.4 and 1.6. Come to Twentymile Creek Backcountry Campsite #93, at mile 1.7. Immediately cross another bridge beyond the campsite. The trail now runs farther above the creek, passing over tributary streams, only to cross Twentymile Creek twice more on bridges before arriving at Proctor Gap and a trail junction at mile 3.0.

Bear right at the trail junction, staying on the Twentymile Trail and enjoying its steady grade. The trail now parallels Proctor Branch. At mile 3.5, the trail steepens, leaving Proctor Branch behind. The final ascent to the A.T. is completed in a series of switchbacks to arrive at Sassafras Gap at mile 4.7.

Turn right on the A.T., climbing out of Sassafras Gap, and come to a side trail on top of Shuckstack at mile 5.0. Turn left and climb a steep grade 0.1 mile to the top of Shuckstack and a fire tower (elevation 4,020 feet). Atop the tower, views abound. The main crest of the Smokies is northward. Fontana Lake covers the flooded valley of the Little Tennessee River to the southeast. From this vantage point, the surrounding Southern Appalachian sea of mountains looks especially rugged.

DIRECTIONS: From Townsend, Tennessee, take US 321 north to the Foothills Parkway. Follow Foothills Parkway west to US 129. Follow US 129 south into North Carolina. Turn left on NC 28. Follow NC 28 for 2.6 miles to the Twentymile Ranger Station, on your left. Park beyond the ranger station and walk up to the gated road to begin your hike on the Twentymile Trail. From the courthouse in Bryson City, North Carolina, take US 19 south for 5.4 miles to NC 28. Follow NC 28 for 30 miles to reach the Twentymile Ranger Station, which will be on your right.

part two

GREAT DAY LOOPS

2

The return trip to the AT will get you huffing and puffing while thinking of all the people that skipped this second view as is evidenced by the much less used trail tread.

Pine Mountain Loop

SCENERY: ✿ ✿ ✿ ✿

DIFFICULTY: ✿ ✿ ✿

TRAIL CONDITIONS: ✿ ✿ ✿ ✿

SOLITUDE: ✿ ✿ ✿ ✿

CHILDREN: ✿ ✿ ✿

DISTANCE: *7.9 miles round-trip*

HIKING TIME: *4:00 round-trip*

OUTSTANDING FEATURES: *pine-oak forest, Abrams Creek*

The two ford crossings of Abrams Creek account for the difficulty rating of this hike. The first ford might be avoided, especially during the summer months when the footlog is restored after winter rains. The second ford is the toughest in the park. But don't let the fords discourage you from taking this scenic loop hike. It is a good opportunity to explore the pine-oak forested western end of the park in a less peopled setting. You'll leave Abrams Creek Ranger Station to cross Abrams for the first time. Then wind up Pine Mountain on a jeep road, descending into Scott Gap. Next, work your way down a south slope to cross the creek again. Follow Abrams Creek on the narrow, twisting Little Bottoms Trail, to return to the ranger station via Cooper Road.

🚶 Start your hike by walking from the parking area. back toward the Abrams Creek Ranger Station. The Rabbit Creek Trail starts at the upper end of the horse pasture. Follow the Rabbit Creek Trail to the first crossing of Abrams Creek at 0.1 mile. Look downstream for the footlog. If it's not there, you'll have to ford the creek. After crossing Abrams Creek, immediately enter an old homesite, with reforesting fields and an old chimney. Start climbing Pine Mountain, switching back at the point of a ridge. Top out on Pine Mountain at mile 2.0, then descend to Scott Gap and a trail junction at mile 2.5.

Near the gap is the Scott Gap trail shelter and a spring to your right. Turn left at the gap on the Hannah Mountain Trail. The trail follows south slopes on its descent to Abrams Creek, with many laurel bushes and pine trees along the route. The second Abrams Creek crossing is at mile 4.3. This is a ford for sure. Use trekking poles or find a stout branch for balance and face upstream as you ford.

PINE MOUNTAIN LOOP

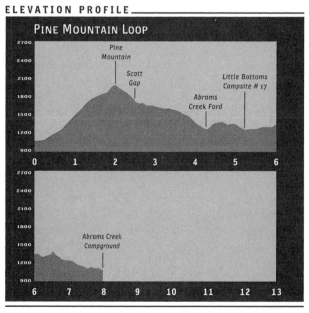

ELEVATION PROFILE

Once across, you'll come to Hatcher Mountain Trail junction. Turn left on the Hatcher Mountain Trail and climb a short distance to another trail junction at mile 4.5. Turn left again and follow the Little Bottoms Trail, which winds far above the Abrams Creek gorge, only to drop down to creek level at Little Bottoms Backcountry Campsite #17, at mile 5.3.

The trail snakes along the creek, then leaves the gorge to top a side ridge at mile 6.5. Wind along a pair of switchbacks and you'll be down at Kingfisher Creek and the Cooper Road Trail junction at mile 6.8. Turn left on Cooper Road Trail to arrive at the Abrams Creek campground at mile 7.9. The parking area is 0.5 mile farther down Abrams Creek Road.

> DIRECTIONS: From Townsend, Tennessee, drive north on US 321. Turn left onto the Foothills Parkway, then left again 18 miles ahead onto US 129 at Chilhowee Lake. Head south 0.5 mile to Happy Valley Road. Turn left on Happy Valley Road, following it 6 miles to Abrams Creek Road. Turn right on Abrams Creek Road and drive 1 mile to the campground, passing the ranger station. Cooper Road Trail starts at the rear of the campground. Park your car in the designated area near the ranger station.

Rich Mountain Loop

SCENERY: ✪ ✪ ✪ ✪
DIFFICULTY: ✪ ✪
TRAIL CONDITIONS: ✪ ✪ ✪ ✪ ✪
SOLITUDE: ✪ ✪ ✪
CHILDREN: ✪ ✪ ✪
DISTANCE: *8.5 miles round-trip*
HIKING TIME: *4:15 round-trip*
OUTSTANDING FEATURES: *old cabin, view of Cades Cove and mountains beyond*

THIS IS A PLEASANT DAY HIKE *that shows Cades Cove from a unique perspective, with a stop by the historic John Oliver cabin thrown in for good measure. Initially you'll stay in the basin of the cove, then climb up Rich Mountain to an inspiring overlook. After you top out on Rich Mountain, with good but interspersed views, you'll circle back down on the Crooked Arm Ridge Trail, completing the loop.*

🥾 Start your hike on the Rich Mountain Loop Trail, rock-hopping over Crooked Arm Branch,

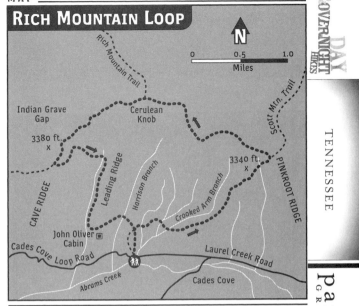

RICH MOUNTAIN LOOP

ELEVATION PROFILE ————

RICH MOUNTAIN LOOP TRAIL

then come to a trail junction at mile 0.5. This is the return point of your loop. Veer left on the Rich Mountain Loop Trail. Cross Harrison Branch as you keep a northwesterly course. At mile 1.2, the John Oliver cabin, built in 1820, will be on your left. Oliver was an early settler of the cove and helped populate it with his many offspring.

The climb begins in earnest when you turn up Martha's Branch and begin switchbacking up Rich Mountain, along Cave Ridge. Your first notable view of the cove opens up on your left at mile 3.0, just as you come to the 3,000-foot level. The Indian Grave Gap Trail junction is at mile 3.4 and offers another cove view.

Turn right and begin a moderate climb on the Indian Grave Gap Trail, reaching the Rich Mountain Trail junction at mile 4.2. Push on up the Indian Grave Gap Trail near the top of Rich Mountain, where a fire tower once stood near the spur trail to your left. The forest cover limits the views now, but the clearing makes an ideal picnic spot.

Start descending Rich Mountain. At mile 5.9, near a clearing for a power line, is the junction with Crooked Arm Ridge Trail. As you begin the trail, keep your eyes raised to enjoy the vista from an overlook. Switchback down toward Cades Cove, crossing Crooked Arm Branch near the base of the mountain.

Complete the loop at mile 8.0, where the trail intersects the Rich Mountain Loop Trail. Follow it 0.5 mile back down to the loop road and the cove you just viewed from above.

DIRECTIONS: From the Townsend "Wye," turn right onto Laurel Creek Road, and follow it for 7.4 miles to the beginning of Cades Cove Loop Road. Park at the beginning of the loop and walk a short way down the loop road to the Rich Mountain Loop Trail, which is on your right.

Finley Cane Loop

> SCENERY: ✿ ✿ ✿ ✿
> DIFFICULTY: ✿ ✿
> TRAIL CONDITIONS: ✿ ✿ ✿ ✿
> SOLITUDE: ✿ ✿ ✿ ✿
> CHILDREN: ✿ ✿ ✿ ✿
> DISTANCE: *8.9 miles round-trip*
> HIKING TIME: *4:15 round-trip*
> OUTSTANDING FEATURES: *old homesites, mountainsides, small creeks*

ALTHOUGH YOU MUST CROSS A ROAD *during this excursion, the trails on this hike are lightly used, offering a pleasantly undulating loop with very little climbing, considering the mountainous setting. First, you will walk among old homesites, the trail gently winding along the side of Turkeypen Ridge. Then you'll follow an old road to the historic Bote Mountain Trail. Finally, the Bote Mountain Trail will lead you to the Finley Cane Trail along the northern base of Bote Mountain to complete your loop.*

🏃 Start your hike along the Turkeypen Ridge Trail, descending from Big Spring Cove to the Crib Gap Trail junction at mile 0.2. Continue on Turkeypen Ridge Trail through an old homesite with relics scattered amid sparse woods. Leave Big Spring Cove to work your way up to a nearly level ridge extending from a flank of Scott Mountain. Drop slightly to cross the most notable creek on the path, Pinkroot Branch, at mile 1.3.

Wind your way along Turkeypen Ridge and notice the differing forest types, determined by the amount of sun exposure. South-facing slopes include various species of pine and mountain laurel, whereas shaded ravines support hemlock and rhododendron. The trail takes a northeast-ward course, sloping down to reach the School-house Gap Trail at mile 3.4.

Turn right on the Schoolhouse Gap Trail and follow it along Spence Branch to Laurel Creek Road at mile 4.5. Turn left on the road, go 50 yards, and cross over to the Bote Mountain Trail. Return to the woods up this former road. Along with the Schoolhouse Gap road-turned-trail,

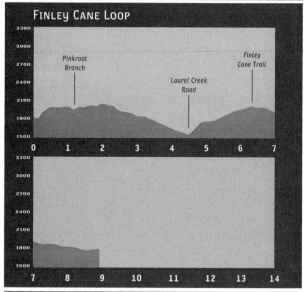

this trail was once part of a plan to connect
Maryville, Tennessee, to the Hazel Creek area.

Stay on the Bote Mountain Trail as you pass
the West Prong Trail at mile 5.7. At mile 6.3,

turn right on the final leg of your loop, the Finley Cane Trail. The woodlands here feature tulip trees, sugar maples, hemlocks, and beeches. Pass Finley Cane's only patch of cane. Crossing many small rills running perpendicular to the trail, you'll rise in and out of watery hollows to a trail junction at mile 8.3. To the right, a horse trail passes under Laurel Creek Road to connect with the Turkeypen Ridge Trail. Continue forward on the Finley Cane Trail to complete your loop to Laurel Creek Road and the Big Spring Cove parking area at mile 8.9.

> **DIRECTIONS**: From Townsend, Tennessee, drive east, turning left at the Townsend "Wye" onto Laurel Creek Road. Head 5.6 miles toward Cades Cove. The Turkeypen Ridge Trail is on your right at the small Big Spring Cove parking area that extends along both sides of the road.

Cucumber Gap Loop

> SCENERY: ✿ ✿ ✿
> DIFFICULTY: ✿ ✿
> TRAIL CONDITIONS: ✿ ✿ ✿ ✿ ✿
> SOLITUDE: ✿ ✿ ✿
> CHILDREN: ✿ ✿ ✿ ✿
> DISTANCE: *5.3 miles round-trip*
> HIKING TIME: *3:00 round-trip*
> OUTSTANDING FEATURES: *river environment, swimming potential*

THIS IS A GREAT HIKE *for those who want more of a woodland stroll rather than a lung-busting mountain climb. Leave Elkmont and cruise up the ultra-attractive Little River valley, where the watercourse tumbles over huge boulders, forming large, clear pools that invite you to take a dip in the cool mountain stream. Leave the Little River for an old railroad grade that gently climbs to a gap, then descends to Jakes Creek valley, where you make your return trip to Elkmont.*

🏃 Start your hike on the Little River Trail, which was moved in the mid 1990s after a flood washed out stretches of the upper section of the old road. Pass through the former Elkmont summer home community on a crumbling asphalt path. The trail soon turns to gravel. The sparkling Little

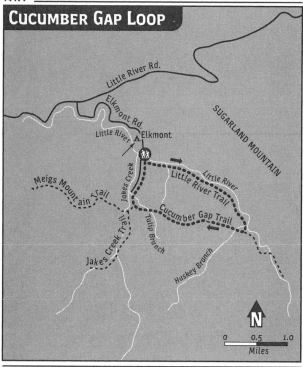

CUCUMBER GAP LOOP

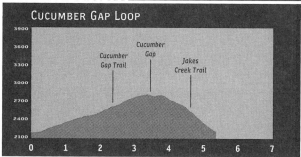

River lies off to the left, always trying to lure you to its banks with attractive shoals, pools, and big rocks ideal for sunning.

At mile 1.0, pass the old parking area—here the path narrows. A bluff pinches the trail to the river in places. In other spots, the Little River is only audible, not visible. At mile 2.0, the waterfall of

Huskey Branch flows beneath a bridge into a large
pool below. Look into the pool for the trout that
lurk in its waters. Keep walking for a bit, coming
to a trail junction at mile 2.3. Turn right here, on
the Cucumber Gap Trail. Ascend on an old railroad grade, crossing Huskey Branch at mile 3.2.
From the trail you will see numerous muscadine
vines. There are more vines growing among the
trees here than in any other part of the park.

The path keeps rising along small feeder
streams of Huskey Branch. Occasionaly, there are
impressive views through the trees to the right.
The path passes just above Cucumber Gap, which
was named for the cucumber tree—itself named
for its green fruit, resembling a mini cucumber.
You can find these fruits trailside in September.
Pass some fairly large beech and hemlock trees
before descending to cross Tulip Branch at
mile 4.4. Come to the wide Jakes Creek Trail
at mile 4.6. Turn right here and descend to a
pole gate at mile 4.9. Enter the Elkmont summer
home community and keep downhill on a crumbling asphalt path to a split in the road at mile
5.2. Turn right here and soon reach the Little
River Trail, completing your loop at mile 5.3.

DIRECTIONS: Drive 4.9 miles from the Sugarland
Visitor Center before turning left into Elkmont. Follow
the paved road 1.3 miles to the Elkmont campground.
Turn left just before the campground check-in station,
and follow the road a short distance to a dead end. The
Little River Trail starts at the end of the gated road.

Boogerman Loop

SCENERY: ✿ ✿ ✿ ✿ ✿
DIFFICULTY: ✿ ✿ ✿
TRAIL CONDITIONS: ✿ ✿ ✿ ✿
SOLITUDE: ✿ ✿ ✿ ✿
CHILDREN: ✿ ✿ ✿
DISTANCE: *7.4 miles round-trip*
HIKING TIME: *3:15 round-trip*
OUTSTANDING FEATURES: *old homesites, huge hemlocks, white pines, tulip trees*

A FOOTLOG CROSSING *is an appropriate beginning for this hike; you'll be quite familiar with them before this loop is over. But first, enjoy the beauty of huge trees, old homesites, and mountain streams on this fulfilling hike, whose trail name was the nickname of the man who owned the land, one Robert "Boogerman" Palmer. There is quite a bit of up and down, and the trail makers, while using old roads, made a few twists and turns to take you by the biggest trees in the area.*

🏃 Cross Cataloochee Creek on a footbridge and enter a stand of white pines. Where the trail splits, stay right and climb a narrow edge along Caldwell Fork. Descend and soon come to the north end of the Boogerman Loop Trail at mile 0.8. Turn left, crossing Caldwell Fork on a footbridge and entering an area of old-growth trees. Leave the cove and climb along a dry ridge before passing through a gap. White pines dominate the slope down to Boogerman's homestead at mile 2.8.

Hike away from the homestead and wind through a series of coves, where the trail intentionally nears many old tulip trees. If you look carefully, you'll notice the tops have been sheared off most of these giants—the result of hundreds of years of rough living in the Smokies. At the last gap, the trail drops straight down and doubles as a streambed in wet weather. At mile 3.8 of your loop, the trail veers right along Snake Branch, around a rock wall, then fords the small stream. Clearings, old fences, and piles of stone are other indicators of homesites along this creek.

More white pines signal your arrival at the Caldwell Fork Trail junction at mile 4.6. Turn

BOOGERMAN LOOP

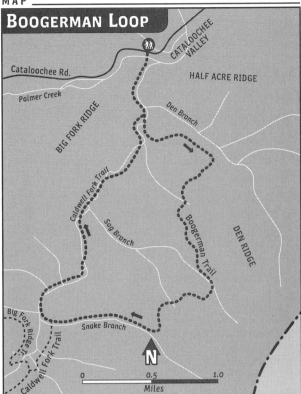

ELEVATION PROFILE

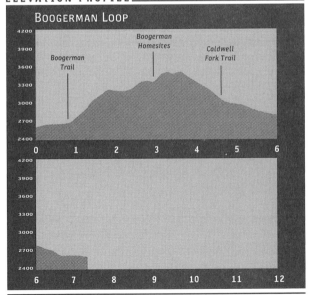

right and head down this picturesque valley. Cross Snake Branch on a footlog and soon start the nine footbridge crossings of Caldwell Fork amid the towering hemlocks. The Caldwell Fork Trail can be muddy and confusing; at stream crossings, the trail frequently splits. Hikers use footbridges and horses ford the creek. Always take the trail headed for higher, drier ground.

These footbridges are a way to appreciate, without getting wet, the normally crystal-clear creek as you descend the valley, with its alternating deep pools and clamoring falls and riffles. At mile 6.6, come again to the northern junction of the Boogerman Loop Trail. Continue down the Caldwell Fork Trail, again passing the needle-carpeted area of white pines. The crossing of Cataloochee Creek on a footbridge at mile 7.4 signals the completion of the loop.

> **DIRECTIONS**: Leave Interstate 40 at exit 20 and drive west on NC 276. Follow it a short distance, then turn right onto Cove Creek Road, which you follow for nearly 6 miles to the park. Two miles beyond the park boundary, turn left onto the paved Cataloochee Road. Follow it 3.1 miles. The Caldwell Fork Trail and its footbridge over Cataloochee Creek will be on your left.

Big Fork Ridge Loop

> SCENERY: ✿ ✿ ✿ ✿
> DIFFICULTY: ✿ ✿ ✿
> TRAIL CONDITIONS: ✿ ✿ ✿ ✿
> SOLITUDE: ✿ ✿ ✿ ✿
> CHILDREN: ✿ ✿ ✿
> DISTANCE: *9.3 miles round-trip*
> HIKING TIME: *5:00 round-trip*
> OUTSTANDING FEATURES: *big trees, old pioneer homestead, Civil War grave site*

BIG TREES ARE THE STARS *of this loop, which starts in lovely Cataloochee Valley. Of course, the numerous old growth giants are complemented by other attractive aspects of Smoky Mountain scenery. Add a visit to a pioneer homestead and you end up with a great day in this national park. Start on the Rough Fork Trail, tracing a clear*

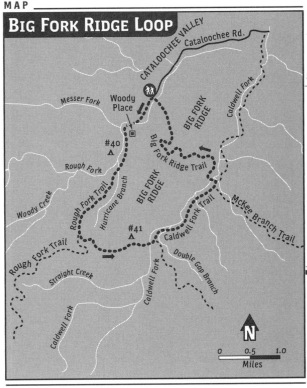

mountain stream. Stop by the Woody Place, then enter the land of the giants, where stately hemlock and oak trees form a forest cathedral. Climb away from Rough Fork to meet the Caldwell Fork Trail. Descend past the "Big Poplars," in truth huge tulip trees, then walk along Caldwell Fork valley. Return over Big Fork Ridge to Cataloochee. This loop has two climbs; neither is particularly long or difficult.

🏃 Start this loop on the Rough Fork Trail. Pass around a pole gate with Rough Fork to the left. Cruise the wide, nearly level track under a forest of maple, white pine, and yellow birch. The valley soon narrows. Cross Rough Fork on a footbridge at 0.5 mile, then twice more soon after. The path opens to a clearing and the Woody Place at 1.0 mile. This wood clapboard structure is worth a tour. A look around will reveal the differing ceiling heights, indicating that the structure was built in stages over time. There is also a springhouse nearby.

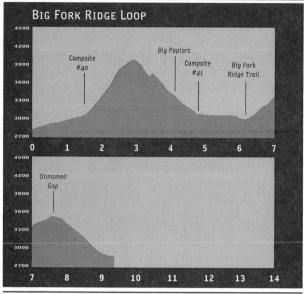

BIG FORK RIDGE LOOP

The Rough Fork Trail continues to enter an old growth woodland of hemlock and northern red oak. Cross Hurricane Creek on a long footbridge and come to Big Hemlock, an appropriately named Backcountry Campsite. A trail leads to the right to access the actual camping area. The path, which has been nearly level to this point, now climbs away from Big Hemlock toward Little Ridge. Big tulip trees grow trailside. There are occasional views of Big Fork Ridge to the left. Top out on Little Ridge just before intersecting the Caldwell Fork Trail at mile 3.0.

Turn left here on the Caldwell Fork Trail and descend through more big trees into the Caldwell Fork valley. At mile 4.1, come to the side trail accessing the behemoth tulip trees, once mistakenly dubbed the "Big Poplars." These trees are huge and take several outstretched arms to encircle. Soon you pass through a former clearing and then reach Caldwell Fork Backcountry Campsite and the Hemphill Bald Trail at mile 4.8. Keep descending along the valley of Caldwell Fork, then reach a side trail leading to the right to reach a grave site at mile 5.9. Up this trail are the graves of two Civil War soldiers who were killed late in the war. Meet the McKee Branch Trail not far beyond the gravesite spur. Keep along Caldwell Fork Trail, which can be muddy in places, just a short distance farther to meet the Big Fork Ridge Trail at mile 6.2.

Make a dry crossing via a footbridge over Caldwell Fork on the Big Fork Ridge Trail, and begin to wind up Big Fork Ridge, reaching a gap at mile 7.6. Descend into the Rough Fork valley. Here you reach a cove and a pioneer homesite, as evidenced by fields being reclaimed by forest. Cross Rough Fork on a footbridge to complete your loop at mile 9.3.

DIRECTIONS: From exit 20 on I-40, head south a short distance on US 276. Turn right onto Cove Creek Road, which you follow nearly 6 miles to enter the park. Two miles beyond the park boundary, turn left onto Cataloochee Road. Follow it to dead end at the Rough Fork Trail, which is at the end of the parking area.

Hyatt Ridge Loop

SCENERY: ☆ ☆ ☆ ☆
DIFFICULTY: ☆ ☆ ☆
TRAIL CONDITIONS: ☆ ☆ ☆ ☆
SOLITUDE: ☆ ☆ ☆ ☆ ☆
CHILDREN: ☆ ☆ ☆
DISTANCE: 7.8 miles round-trip
HIKING TIME: 4:15 round-trip
OUTSTANDING FEATURES: isolation, old growth forest

THIS LOOP HIKE TAKES YOU AWAY FROM Straight Fork Road into the seldom visited high country on Hyatt Ridge. Take the side trail to McGhee Spring Backcountry Campsite for lunch (this adds 1.8 miles to the hike), then return via the Beech Gap Trail to Straight Fork. A short walk along the lightly used Straight Fork Road will complete your loop.

🚶 Start your trip on the Hyatt Ridge Trail, beyond the gate on an old railroad grade, crossing Hyatt Creek at mile 0.7. Continue to ascend

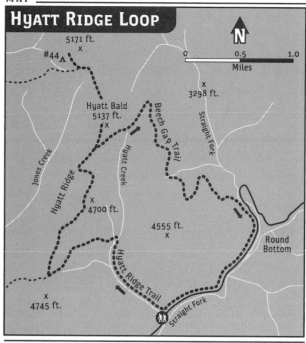

HYATT RIDGE LOOP

N

5171 ft.
X

#44 ▲

Hyatt Bald
5137 ft.
X

X
3298 ft.

Beech Gap Trail

Straight Fork

Jones Creek

Hyatt Ridge

Hyatt Creek

X
4700 ft.

4555 ft.
X

Round
Bottom

Hyatt Ridge Trail

X
4745 ft.

Straight Fork

0   0.5   1.0
Miles

steeply through second growth forest up the side
of Hyatt Ridge. Come to Low Gap and a trail
junction atop Hyatt Ridge (elevation 4,400 feet)
at mile 1.9. Straight ahead is the Enloe Creek
Trail. Many spruce grow on this ridge.

Turn right, remaining on the Hyatt Ridge
Trail. Climb out of the gap for another 0.5 mile
and come to an area of old-growth forest. Veer
left, then make a sharp right turn to climb
northeasterly on Hyatt Bald, now wooded with a
grassy understory, a reminder of its former state.

At mile 3.6, you come to another trail junction. This 0.9-mile trail leads to McGhee Spring
Backcountry Campsite #44. At an elevation of
5,040 feet, this makes an excellent lunch spot
located by a perennial spring in a mountain
glade. To continue the Hyatt Ridge Loop, turn
right on the Beech Gap Trail (once known as the
Hyatt Bald Trail). Sections of this trail have tall,
waving grasses under the trees.

Descend gradually on the Beech Gap Trail,
maintaining a northeasterly course. At mile 4.4,

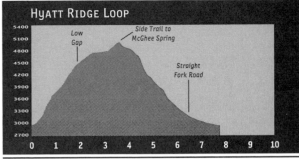

in a grassy gap, make a switchback to the right, leaving the ridge top. Wind your way southward, passing the upper reaches of Grass Branch at mile 5.4. Soon the waters of Straight Fork hum in the distance as the trail skirts more small branches, to arrive at Straight Fork Road, at mile 6.5.

Turn right on Straight Fork Road, following its namesake stream down into Big Cove and Cherokee Reservation territory. This lightly used road actually makes for pleasant walking. You may encounter the occasional fisherman along the stream. Arrive at the Hyatt Ridge trailhead on your right at mile 7.8 to complete the loop.

DIRECTIONS: From the Oconaluftee Visitor Center, drive 1 mile south to Big Cove Road. Turn left on Big Cove Road and follow it 10.4 miles through the Cherokee Reservation to the park boundary. Drive 2.5 miles beyond the boundary to the Hyatt Ridge trailhead, on your left.

Smokemont Loop

SCENERY: ✿ ✿ ✿ ✿
DIFFICULTY: ✿ ✿
TRAIL CONDITIONS: ✿ ✿ ✿ ✿ ✿
SOLITUDE: ✿ ✿ ✿
CHILDREN: ✿ ✿ ✿ ✿
DISTANCE: 5.4 miles round-trip
HIKING TIME: 2:45 round-trip
OUTSTANDING FEATURES: good family day hike through history and woods

THIS LOOP HIKE LEADS AWAY from the popular Smokemont campground along Bradley Fork, then upward along the southern

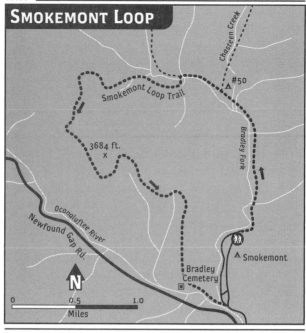

reaches of Richland Mountain. The trail winds back down near the Oconaluftee River, past the Bradley Cemetery, returning to the Smokemont campground.

🏃 Start your loop hike on the Bradley Fork Trail, at the rear of the Smokemont campground. Pass an outbuilding, then a side road on your right leading to the water supply for the campground at mile 0.3. Open areas with thin forest cover indicate former homesites along the trail. At mile 1.0, cross a wide wooden bridge over Chasteen Creek, then come to the Chasteen Creek Trail junction. Press forward through the junction and come to the Smokemont Loop Trail junction at mile 1.6.

Turn left on the Smokemont Loop Trail, crossing Bradley Fork on a long footbridge, then a smaller branch on another footbridge. The narrow foot trail immediately switchbacks right, then left, swings around a knob on the way up

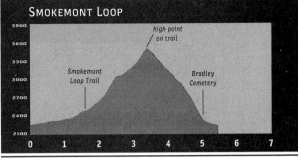

SMOKEMONT LOOP

Richland Mountain, and reaches the crest at mile
2.7. The white noise of the Oconaluftee River
accompanies you on your southward journey
along Richland Mountain.

The trail reaches its high point, nearly
3,500 feet, at mile 3.4. A couple of downed
logs invite a rest here. The trail begins to wind
down the slope of Richland Mountain, alternately flanked by open woods and thick rhododendron. At mile 5.0, Bradley Cemetery
appears on your right, farther along the trail.
Continue down to a jeep road that used to loop
through a now closed section of the Smokemont
campground, and turn right to reach a side trail
to the cemetery. Climb a small hill to the cemetery. Worn-down stones marking the graves of
settlers whose names are lost to time stand
beside gravestones with legible names.

Return to the jeep road and follow it over
Bradley Fork on an old stone bridge back to the
Smokemont campground at mile 5.4, completing
your loop. The Bradley Fork trailhead is to your
left at the rear of the campground.

DIRECTIONS: From the Oconaluftee Visitor Center,
drive 3.2 miles north on Newfound Gap Road. Turn right
into the Smokemont campground on a bridge over the
Oconaluftee River. Veer left and pass the campground
check-in station. The Bradley Fork Trail starts at the gated
jeep road at the right rear of the campground as you enter.

Indian Creek Loop

SCENERY: ☆ ☆ ☆ ☆

DIFFICULTY: ☆ ☆ ☆

TRAIL CONDITIONS: ☆ ☆ ☆ ☆

SOLITUDE: ☆ ☆ ☆

CHILDREN: ☆ ☆ ☆

DISTANCE: *12.4 miles round-trip*

HIKING TIME: *6:15 round-trip*

OUTSTANDING FEATURES: *quiet ridge, Indian Creek Falls*

THIS LOOP HIKE FOLLOWS DEEP CREEK *to Indian Creek, past Indian Creek Falls, then climbs to Martins Gap. You return via the quiet Sunkota Ridge Trail with its drier forest, back to Deep Creek and its accompanying riverine habitat. You can appreciate the*

MAP

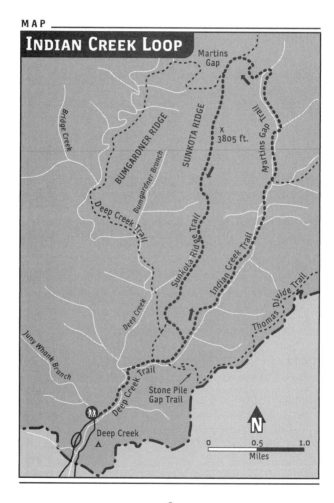

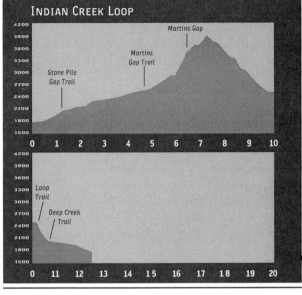

*biological diversity of the Smokies on this fairly easy trek through a
relatively small area.*

🚶 Start your hike on the Deep Creek Trail at the
end of Deep Creek Road just beyond the Deep
Creek campground. Follow an old gravel road,
crossing Deep Creek on a bridge en route to the
Indian Creek Trail junction at mile 0.7. Turn
right on the Indian Creek Trail, coming to
Indian Creek Falls at mile 0.8. A short side trail
on your right leads to the base of the falls. At
mile 1.2, the Stone Pile Gap Trail goes right.
Then, at mile 1.5, the Loop Trail heads up
Sunkota Ridge to your left. Stay on the Indian
Creek Trail, heading north.

A number of pioneer homesites appear
alongside the water between several bridged
crossings of Indian Creek. A gradual climb leads
to the Deeplow Gap Trail junction at mile 3.6.
Continue following the Indian Creek Trail to its
end at mile 4.6, located at a road turnaround
near Estes Branch. The park service arbitrarily
starts the Martins Gap Trail at this point.

Keep hiking through the turnaround, and
begin the Martins Gap Trail. Within the next

half-mile, you'll cross Indian Creek three times on footbridges before switchbacking up the side of Sunkota Ridge to arrive at Martins Gap at mile 6.4. Martins Gap, a sag on Sunkota Ridge, has a four-way trail intersection. Turn left on the serene Sunkota Ridge Trail. Sunkota is the pioneer pronunciation of an Indian word meaning apple.

Climb out of the gap to the loop's high point at mile 7.2, and begin a slow descent, winding along the ridge top and its flanks. At mile 10.2, come to the end of the Sunkota Ridge Trail and the Loop Trail junction. Turn right on the Loop Trail down to the Deep Creek Trail at mile 10.7. Follow Deep Creek Trail downstream over three bridges to the Indian Creek Trail at mile 11.7. Return to the trailhead on the short section of the Deep Creek Trail you traversed earlier to the Deep Creek trailhead at mile 12.4.

DIRECTIONS: From the Oconaluftee Visitor Center, take US 441 south to Cherokee, North Carolina. Turn right on US 19 to Bryson City, North Carolina. Turn right at the Swain County Courthouse onto Everett Street and carefully follow the signs through town to the Deep Creek campground. The Deep Creek Trail is at the back of the campground.

Goldmine Loop

SCENERY: ✫ ✫ ✫ ✫
DIFFICULTY: ✫
TRAIL CONDITIONS: ✫ ✫ ✫ ✫
SOLITUDE: ✫ ✫ ✫ ✫ ✫
CHILDREN: ✫ ✫ ✫ ✫ ✫
DISTANCE: *3.3 miles round-trip*
HIKING TIME: *1:45 round-trip*
OUTSTANDING FEATURES: *Fontana Lake, Lakeview tunnel, homesites*

THIS SHORT LOOP HIKE TRAVERSES *a seldom visited area of the Smokies. Beginning at Lakeview Drive, you hike down to Fontana Lake. The trail moves away from the lake, passing several old homesites along the way, then returns to Lakeview Drive through*

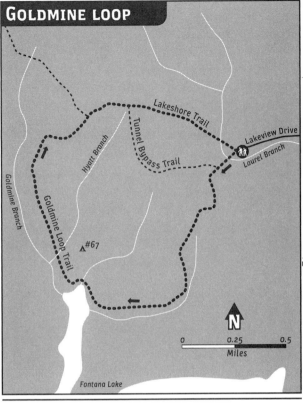

GOLDMINE LOOP

Lakeshore Trail

Lakeview Drive

Tunnel Bypass Trail

Hyatt Branch

Laurel Branch

Goldmine Branch

Goldmine Loop Trail

▲#67

N

| 0 | 0.25 | 0.5 |

Miles

Fontana Lake

ELEVATION PROFILE

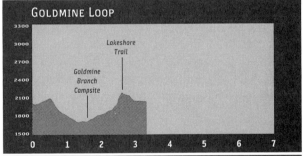

GOLDMINE LOOP

Lakeshore
Trail

Goldmine
Branch
Campsite

*the Lakeview tunnel. Several old roads and trails branch off the
Goldmine loop, so watch your direction.*

🚶 The loop hike starts near the parking area at
the end of Lakeview Drive. With your back to the
parking area, begin your hike on the Tunnel

Bypass Trail, just across the road and to the left of the parking area. Once on the trail, descend briefly through a rhododendron thicket and then climb up to a small gap at mile 0.3. An old trail lies below and leads to the same gap. Proceed forward through the gap, skirting a knob to arrive at another gap and a trail junction on a modest ridge at mile 0.5.

Turn left on the Goldmine Loop Trail and descend down a ridge on the narrow path. Come to an old road that parallels Tunnel Branch and veer right. The forest is more closed-in here than on the ridgetop. The old road turns away from Tunnel Branch and comes to Fontana Lake at mile 1.3.

Intersect another road that swings around and over a tiny creek, then passes over Hyatt Branch via stone culverts. Come to the side trail leading to Goldmine Branch Backcountry Campsite #67, at mile 1.7. The campsite is located in an open homesite a few hundred yards up the side trail.

The Goldmine Loop Trail again crosses Goldmine Branch on a culvert, then becomes muddy. Beyond the muddy area, the trail briefly leaves the road and skirts to the right of a homesite. The Goldmine Loop Trail rejoins the old road to reach a second homesite at mile 2.2. A stone chimney stands near the trail. Swing past the homesite in a rhododendron tunnel to emerge at the top of the hollow. The road continues forward but the trail makes a sharp right up the side of a ridge to a saddle. Next, the pathway veers left for a short but steep climb to intersect the Lakeshore Trail at mile 2.6.

Turn right on the Lakeshore Trail and, within a scant 100 yards, you'll come to a junction with the Tunnel Bypass Trail. Pass forward through the junction and come to the Lakeview tunnel at mile 2.9. Walk the 0.2-mile-long tunnel and emerge near Lakeview Drive. Pass beyond the gate and complete your 3.3-mile loop.

Twentymile Loop

SCENERY: ✿ ✿ ✿ ✿

DIFFICULTY: ✿ ✿

TRAIL CONDITIONS: ✿ ✿ ✿

SOLITUDE: ✿ ✿ ✿ ✿ ✿

CHILDREN: ✿ ✿ ✿ ✿

DISTANCE: *7.4 miles round-trip*

HIKING TIME: *3:45 round-trip*

OUTSTANDING FEATURES: *waterfall, mountain streams, deep woods*

THIS STREAMSIDE LOOP HIKE *never gets too far from the sound of falling water, one of the key ingredients of Smokies ambiance. This is one of the most rewarding out-of-the-way trips in the park. The hike travels along Twentymile Creek, then veers left on the Wolf Ridge Trail with Moore Spring Branch, a fine trout stream, as your noisy companion. Turn east on the Twentymile Loop Trail into deep woods, over Long Hungry Ridge, and down to the Twentymile Trail. Follow Twentymile Creek as it cascades down toward Cheoah Lake.*

🚶 Start your loop on the Twentymile Trail, following it to mile 0.6, then hike over the bridged crossing of Moore Spring Branch to the Wolf Ridge Trail junction. Turn left on the Wolf Ridge Trail to cross Moore Spring Branch on footlogs three times in the first half mile. Cross Moore Spring Branch without the benefit of footlogs at mile 1.3 and 1.5.

At mile 1.6, the Twentymile Loop Trail junction, turn right. The Twentymile Loop Trail heads east, fording Moore Spring Branch yet again, then ascends toward a gap. After some meandering up the side of Long Hungry Ridge, the trail passes through a sag in the ridge at mile 3.2, where a deteriorating sign once announced the gap's name.

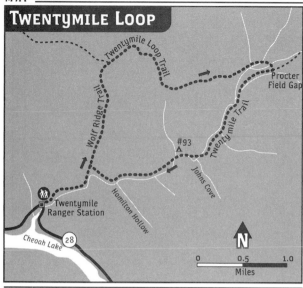

TWENTYMILE LOOP

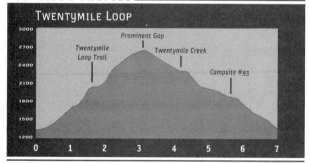

The Twentymile Loop Trail soon slopes sharply down heavily wooded Long Hungry Ridge, an ideal place to pause and absorb the essence of a southern Appalachian forest. Ford Twentymile Creek at mile 4.2, then cross a level area before rising to Proctor Gap and a trail junction at mile 4.4.

Turn right on the Twentymile Trail, following its namesake, Twentymile Creek, downstream. Just after crossing a wide bridge, come to Twentymile Creek Backcountry Campsite #93, at mile 5.7. Cross two more bridges in short succession to arrive at the side trail for Twentymile Cascades at mile 6.7. Take the side trail to view the waterfall that descends in stages. At mile 6.8, your previous turnoff, the Wolf Ridge Trail joins the path from the right. Follow the Twentymile Trail past the horse barn and back to the trailhead at mile 7.4.

DIRECTIONS: From Townsend, Tennessee, drive west on US 321 and turn left onto Foothills Parkway. Follow Foothills Parkway west to US 129. Follow US 129 south into North Carolina. Turn left on NC 28. Follow NC 28 for 2.6 miles to Twentymile Ranger Station, on your left. Park beyond the ranger station, walk up to the gated road, and begin your hike on the Twentymile Trail. From the courthouse in Bryson City, North Carolina, take US 19 south for 5.4 miles to NC 28. Turn right on NC 28 and go 30 miles to Twentymile Ranger Station, on your right.

part three

GREAT OVERNIGHT LOOPS

The return trip to the AT will get you huffing and puffing, while thinking of all the people that skipped this second view as is evidenced by the much less used trail tread.

Fontana *Overnight Loop*

SCENERY: ✿ ✿ ✿ ✿ ✿

TRAIL CONDITION: ✿ ✿ ✿ ✿

CHILDREN: ✿ ✿ ✿

DIFFICULTY: ✿ ✿

SOLITUDE: ✿ ✿ ✿

DISTANCE: *4.5, 8.9, 8.1 miles each day*

HIKING TIME: *2:45, 5:00, 4:15 each day*

OUTSTANDING FEATURES: *lakeside camping, pioneer history, good initiation backpack*

IF YOU LIKE A COMBINATION *of mountains and lakes, this moderate hike is for you and any younger or inexperienced backpackers you may wish to bring along, though the mileages may be a bit challenging for the uninitiated. Start your trip on a boat that takes you on the pleasure ride from Fontana Marina to Hazel Creek. Hike up a modest grade on the Hazel Creek Trail through a valley steeped in settler and logging history to camp at Sugar Fork, one of the Smokies' best campsites. Then backtrack down Hazel Creek to cross over into the Eagle Creek watershed on the a new section of the Lakeshore Trail to camp on Fontana Lake, and simultaneously enjoy a tumbling stream and a mountain rimmed lake. On the way back, pass more human history, still on the Lakeshore Trail, to intersect the Appalachian Trail, and walk over Fontana Dam, the highest in the East, to the Fontana Marina.*

🚶 Before you leave, contact Fontana Marina at (828) 498-2211, extension 277, to arrange for a one-way shuttle; you will hike back to the marina. Start your trip at the mouth of Hazel Creek on the Hazel Creek Trail. Pass Proctor Creek Backcountry Campsite #86, at mile 0.5. Soon cross Hazel Creek on a wide bridge. The house beside the creek, the Calhoun Place, is owned and used by the park. The new portion of the Lakeshore Trail heads west past the house. Remember this spot, as you will be backtracking to here. Hike along the jeep road and watch for the many signs of the homestead and logging days.

As you hike, the scenic mountain stream is often visible and makes itself heard even when it cannot be seen. Cross two wide bridges before arriving at Sawdust Pile Backcountry Campsite

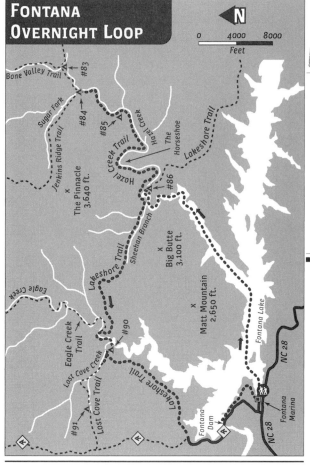

#85, on your righ tat mile 3.3. Span two more bridges before coming to a trail junction at mile 4.5. To your right, just across the bridge over Sugar Fork, is the Sugar Fork Backcountry Campsite #84, at an elevation of 2,160 feet. This is your first night's destination. Nestled between Sugar Fork and Hazel Creeks, this level campsite beneath the pines makes an ideal base camp for the angler or amateur archaeologist. Consider walking up to Bone Valley or up Sugar Fork on the Jenkins Ridge Trail, exploring Hazel Creek Valley's past. But, leave anything you find.

Start day two by backtracking downstream along Hazel Creek, appreciating the many cascades

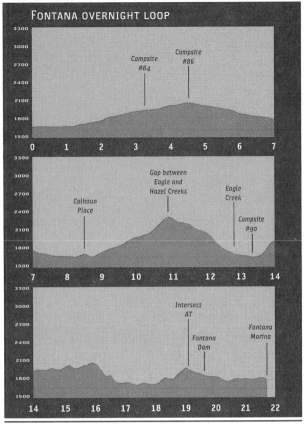

FONTANA OVERNIGHT LOOP

of this stream that exemplify the beauty of this national park. At mile 8.4 of your loop hike, keep on the west side of Hazel Creek on the Lakeshore Trail, as it passes by the Calhoun Place. Climb along a bluff only to descend again. Remnants of the old community of Proctor, including chimneys, walls, foundations, are very evident along the valley of Sheehan Branch. You can visit the Proctor Cemetery via a side trail at mile 8.9. The lower part of this valley was known as Possum Hollow. Continue up an old wagon road along an ever-diminishing watercourse to reach a gap at nearly 2,400 feet at mile 10.9. From here, the Lakeshore Trail was graded by park personnel to level the footpath. Descend through hickory-oak and pine woods. Many pines are dead from Southern pine beetle infestations in the early 2000s. Watch for boulders on the ridgeline as you traverse small gaps. Briefly travel along a streamlet to emerge along Eagle Creek at mile 12.8. The rushing sounds contrast with the quiet woods of the ridge top. Turn left to descend along Eagle Creek and cross a metal frame bridge. Veer right, and the lake comes into view on your left. Pass over Lost Cove Creek on a footlog to arrive at Lost Cove Backcountry Campsite #90 (elevation 1,760 feet) at mile 13.4. This is your second night's destination. This popular campsite extends out beyond the trees and offers fishing and swimming in both Fontana Lake and mountain streams nearby.

Start day three by finding the Lost Cove Trail. As you look out on the lake from the campsite, the Lost Cove Trail will be uphill and to your right. Follow the trail 0.4 mile to the Lakeshore Trail junction. Turn left on the Lakeshore Trail. This portion of the Lakeshore Trail has many old roads and trails leading off it, so make sure you stay on the right path. Fontana Lake will be on your left the whole way.

The trail follows a familiar pattern: up and around a point of a ridge, and down into a creek-filled hollow; up the side of a ridge and over the point, and down again into a hollow. At mile 16.7 of your loop hike, intersect a former road, Old NC 28. It still has some junker cars from the 1930s nearby. Homesites and other evidence of human habitation are all around this section of trail. Leave the old road at mile 18.5, and climb to another old road that leads to Fontana Dam Road at mile 19.2. Intersect the Appalachian Trail at the Lakeshore Trail parking area.

Road walk and reach the north side of Fontana Dam at mile 19.7. Cross Fontana Dam, appreciating the immensity of the project and the views of Fontana Lake. Follow the Appalachian Trail to the left away from Fontana Dam Road and reenter woodland. Pass a trail shelter known as the Fontana "Hilton," because it is so fancy. After running a low ridgeline through thick woods, the A.T. crosses a road leading to the marina. The marina is a short distance downhill to your left. Turn left on the road and complete your loop at mile 21.5.

DIRECTIONS: From Townsend, Tennessee, take US 321 north to the Foothills Parkway. Follow the Foothills Parkway to US 129. Turn South on US 129 into North Carolina. Turn left on NC 28, passing Fontana Village. Go 1.5 miles past the Fontana Village entrance and turn left at the sign to Fontana Dam. Next, turn right at the sign to Fontana Village Marina a short distance away. From Bryson City, North Carolina, take US 19 south to NC 28. Follow NC 28 for nearly 25 miles to turn right at the sign to Fontana Dam, then right again to Fontana Village Marina.

Chasteen Creek *Overnight Loop*

SCENERY: ✪ ✪ ✪ ✪ ✪
TRAIL CONDITION: ✪ ✪ ✪ ✪
CHILDREN: ✪ ✪
DIFFICULTY: ✪ ✪ ✪
SOLITUDE: ✪ ✪ ✪
DISTANCE: *3.5, 8.7, 5.2, miles each day*
HIKING TIME: *2:00, 4:15, 2:30 each day*
OUTSTANDING FEATURES: *waterfalls, bear country*

THIS LOOP TRAVELS WATERCOURSES *and ridges of the Bradley Fork watershed. Leave Smokemont Campground and make your way up Bradley Fork, only to turn up Chasteen Creek, where a waterfall awaits along a side trail. Continue to the upper reaches of the stream and overnight at Upper Chasteen Creek Backcountry Campsite. The next day, climb through mountainside woodlands to reach Hughes Ridge. Here, rhododendron and altitude-loving Fraser fir trees line the trail. Make a pleasant cruise in the high country before dropping down Taywa Creek and returning to Bradley Fork. Head up Bradley Fork to camp at Cabin Flats, one of the Smokies' most notorious campsites, due to the frequency of bear encounters in the past. Worry not, as bearproof food storage cables have been installed here, as at all other Smokies campsites. Bradley Fork is simply beautiful here, and is great for wading, fishing, or simply peering into the crystalline waters. Also, in June, backpackers can achieve a big bloom "triple crown," as flame azalea, mountain laurel, and rhododendron flower alongside the trails.*

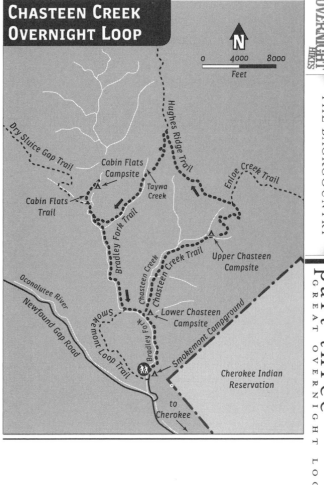

CHASTEEN CREEK OVERNIGHT LOOP

N

0   4000   8000

Feet

Dry Sluice Gap Trail

Hughes Ridge Trail

Enloe Creek Trail

Cabin Flats Campsite

Taywa Creek

Cabin Flats Trail

Bradley Fork Trail

Chasteen Creek

Chasteen Creek Trail

Upper Chasteen Campsite

Oconalutee River

Newfound Gap Road

Smokemont Loop Trail

Bradley Fork

Lower Chasteen Campsite

Smokemont Campground

Cherokee Indian Reservation

to Cherokee

🚶 Leave the Smokemont Campground. Bradley Fork flows, dashes, and splashes along the Bradley Fork Trail, where mossy boulders and ferns lie beneath the forest, with many locust and tulip trees taking over former clearings. Try to imagine the homesites that once occupied these flats. Cross a wooden bridge over Chasteen Creek at mile 1.0. Just beyond this crossing is the Chasteen Creek Trail junction. Above this small clearing is Lower Chasteen Creek Backcountry Campsite.

As you turn right onto the Chasteen Creek Trail, the trailbed narrows. Bridge Chasteen Creek again at mile 1.4. The gradient steepens

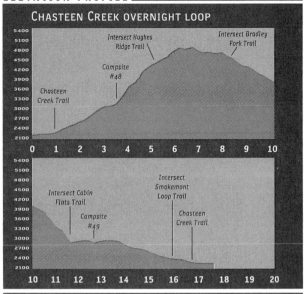

CHASTEEN CREEK OVERNIGHT LOOP

Intersect Hughes Ridge Trail

Intersect Bradley Fork Trail

Campsite #48

Chasteen Creek Trail

Intersect Cabin Flats Trail

Campsite #49

Intersect Smokemont Loop Trail

Chasteen Creek Trail

beneath the forest, which has an occasional grassy understory. Other areas are thick with rhododendron. The trail splits near a hitching post at mile 2.0. A side path leads to Chasteen Creek and a 20-foot cascade tumbling over rocks. Now the path drifts away from the creek, crossing a major feeder branch. Watch for a low-flow cascade emanating from another side stream and passing under the trail. Reach the campsite at mile 3.5 after a short climb. This tiered sloping site, with more emphasis on slope than tier, stands at 3,300 feet. Small streams seemingly encircle the camp.

Start day two by continuing up the Chasteen Creek Trail, which steepens and narrows to a single-track footpath. The white noise of falling streams becomes noticeably absent as you achieve a drier ridgeline, where flame azaleas bloom in June. Small seeps up here may be dry during later summer and fall—water up before you leave the campsite. The path switchbacks among mountain laurel and offers glimpses to the south and west. Reach the Hughes Ridge Trail at mile 5.0 of your loop hike. Turn left here and begin heading mostly uphill in attractive mixed woodland that includes red spruce. Intersect the Enloe Creek Trail at mile 5.4, and ascend away from the gap to reach a high point at mile 6.1—you are now nearly 5,100 feet. Descend through a dark spruce copse, enjoying the moderate nature of the path. The high-country ramble continues to reach an attractive junction at mile 7.9, where grass grows amid the trees. Turn left here, descending on the upper Bradley Fork Trail around the point of a ridge, at times tunneling through rhododendron. Bridge Taywa Creek the first time at mile 9.8 and keep steadily descending. Notice a waterfall with a "Stream Closed" sign. This fall is a barrier to rainbow trout, and the park service wants to keep the upper reaches of Taywa Creek the domain of the native brook trout, so fishing for "brookies" above the fall is prohibited.

The path turns away from Taywa Creek before reaching a trail junction and a resting bench at mile 11.1. Bradley Fork is crashing on the far side of the rhododendron. Here, pick up the Cabin Flats Trail and immediately cross Bradley Fork on an impressive trestle bridge that you will appreciate if the water is high. Cross Tennessee Branch on a footbridge, just beyond which lies the Dry Sluice Gap Trail junction at mile 11.5.

The Cabin Flats Trail winds along the west side of the Bradley Fork valley before descending into Cabin Flats proper at mile 12.2, after a sharp right turn. This is the location of Cabin Flats Backcountry Campsite #49. Over the years, this campsite has been closed for periods due to bear activity. Bear or a human, I would come here to enjoy the beauty of the stream and woods. However, the flood of spring 2003 blew the creekside wide open and much rock is exposed. As old as these mountains are, they just keep changing.

Start day three of your loop hike by backtracking 1.1 miles on the Cabin Flats Trail to reach the Bradley Fork Trail. Keep descending along Bradley Fork, appreciating more of this superlative watercourse on an easy downgrade. Intersect the Smokemont Loop Trail at mile 15.8 of your loop hike. Soon intersect the Chasteen Creek Trail, then retrace your steps the last mile of the hike to reach Smokemont and the end of the trail at mile 17.4.

DIRECTIONS: From the Oconaluftee Visitor Center, drive 3.2 miles north on Newfound Gap Road to Smokemont campground. Turn right into Smokemont campground on a bridge over the Oconaluftee River. Veer left and pass the campground check-in station. The Bradley Fork Trail starts at the gated jeep road at the right rear of the campground.

Little River *Overnight Loop*

SCENERY: ✿ ✿ ✿ ✿
DIFFICULTY: ✿ ✿ ✿
TRAIL CONDITIONS: ✿ ✿ ✿ ✿
SOLITUDE: ✿ ✿ ✿
CHILDREN: ✿ ✿ ✿
DISTANCE: *6.1, 7.6, 5.8 miles each day*
HIKING TIME: *3:15, 4:00, 3:00 each day*
OUTSTANDING FEATURES: *views, attractive streams, multiple environments*

THIS OVERNIGHT LOOP FOLLOWS *the Little River deep into the heart of the Smokies, where you will camp in the shadow of Clingmans Dome. Then you ascend Sugarland Mountain via the Rough Creek Trail and camp in a boulder field at the little-used Medicine Branch Bluff campsite. This trip offers creekside and ridgeline camping with a fair amount of climbing in between.*

🚶 Start your camping trip on the Little River Trail, on a gentle railroad grade. Pass the remains of the Elkmont vacation home enclave. The cascading Little River offers an ever-changing water show to your left. The stream crashes amid rocks, only to gather in large pools that fall again in a white, frothy mix of water and air. At mile 2.0, Huskey Branch enters the Little River in a fall above the trail, which bridges the small creek. The Cucumber Gap Trail comes in from the west at mile 2.3.

M A P

THE BACKCOUNTRY

&OVERNIGHT
DAY
Hikes

part three
GREAT OVERNIGHT LOOPS

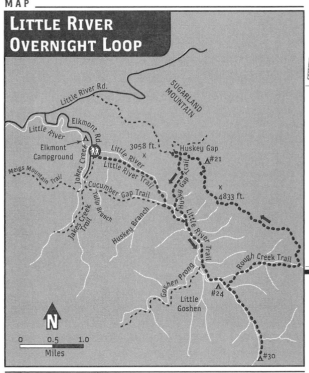

LITTLE RIVER OVERNIGHT LOOP

Little River Rd.

SUGARLAND MOUNTAIN

Little River

Elkmont Rd.

Elkmont Campground

3058 ft. ×

Huskey Gap

△#21

Little River

Little River Trail

Meigs Mountain Trail

Jakes Creek

Cucumber Gap Trail

Huskey Gap Trail

× 4833 ft.

Jakes Creek Trail

Tulip Branch

Huskey Branch

Little River Trail

Rough Creek Trail

Goshen Prong

△ #24

Little Goshen

△#30

N

0   0.5   1.0
Miles

ELEVATION PROFILE

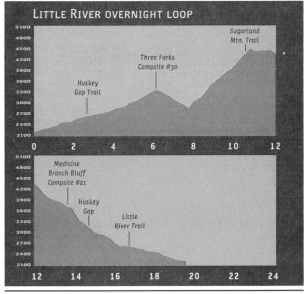

LITTLE RIVER OVERNIGHT LOOP

Huskey Gap Trail

Three Forks Campsite #30

Sugarland Mtn. Trail

5100
4800
4500
4200
3900
3600
3300
3000
2700
2400
2100

0   2   4   6   8   10   12

Medicine Branch Bluff Campsite #21

Huskey Gap

Little River Trail

5100
4800
4500
4200
3900
3600
3300
3000
2700
2400
2100

12   14   16   18   20   22   24

Continue up the Little River, crossing it on a wide bridge just before the Huskey Gap Trail junction at mile 2.7. Stay on the east bank of the Little River, crossing several small feeder streams originating on Sugarland Mountain, and reach a wide flat near the confluence of Goshen Prong and the Little River at mile 3.7. The Goshen Prong Trail bears right; stay on the Little River Trail to reach Rough Creek Backcountry Campsite #24, at mile 4.5.

The Little River trail becomes somewhat rockier as it passes the Rough Creek trail junction, just beyond the campsite. Look for the even spacing of old railroad ties. Keep on the Little River Trail, crossing Meigs Post Prong at mile 5.7, where the remains of an old railroad bridge lie about the creek bed.

Cross what's left of the Little River at mile 6.1, where another old railroad bridge is particularly evident, to arrive at Three Forks Backcountry Campsite #30. At elevation 3,400 feet, this former logging camp is your first night's destination. The high country streams that border this grassy area on three sides are populated with native brook trout.

Start day two by backtracking 1.6 miles down the Little River Trail to meet the Rough Creek Trail at mile 7.7. Turn right and begin climbing the Rough Creek Trail, which also follows an old railroad bed, through second-growth forest. As you climb, notice the various remnants of railroad days. After crossing Rough Creek three times, the trail runs north to intersect the Sugarland Mountain Trail on the narrow ridge at mile 10.5.

Turn left on the Sugarland Mountain Trail. Meander along the ridgetop, staying near 4,500 feet in elevation for the next 1.7 miles, before descending around the southern side of a knob on Sugarland Mountain. After working past a point in the ridge, veer into the Big Medicine Branch hollow. The Medicine Branch Bluff Backcountry Campsite #21, is in a boulder field at mile 13.7. This site is your second night's destination. This lightly used site, at 3,780 feet, is on a fair slope, but a few flat tent sites hide among the boulders. Water can be obtained from the small stream flowing at the base of the hollow.

To begin day three, continue northwest on the Sugarland Mountain Trail. At mile 14.7 of the loop is a junction with the Huskey Gap Trail. Turn left on the Huskey Gap Trail, an old pre-park crossroads, descending past the drainages of Big Medicine Branch and Phoebe Branch to enter a wide, flat area in the vicinity of the Little River. Arrive at the Little River Trail just after crossing Sugar Orchard Branch at mile 16.8.

Head down the Little River Trail, once again passing the Cucumber Gap Trail at mile 17.2. Walk along the west bank of the river to arrive at the trailhead, and the end of your loop, at mile 18.5.

DIRECTIONS: Drive 4.9 miles from the Sugarland Visitor Center, then turn left into Elkmont. Follow the paved road 1.3 miles to the Elkmont campground. Turn left just before the campground check-in station and follow the road a short distance to a dead end. The Little River Trail starts at the end of the gated road.

Maddron Bald *Overnight Loop*

SCENERY: ✿ ✿ ✿ ✿ ✿
DIFFICULTY: ✿ ✿ ✿
TRAIL CONDITIONS: ✿ ✿ ✿ ✿
SOLITUDE: ✿ ✿ ✿ ✿
CHILDREN: ✿ ✿
DISTANCE: *4.8, 6.2, 6.8 miles each day*
HIKING TIME: *2:45, 3:45, 3:55 each day*
OUTSTANDING FEATURES: *Henwallow Falls, old growth forest, Maddron Bald views*

THIS TWO-NIGHT TRIP *is one of if not the best backpacking loops in the entire park! First, hike along the lower reaches of Gabes Mountain, passing Henwallow Falls, and enter virgin woodland to camp at Sugar Cove. Then head up the Maddron Bald Trail to Albright Grove, which contains some of the park's largest trees. Camp along a resonant*

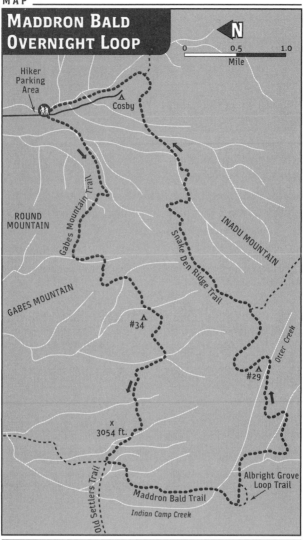

MADDRON BALD
OVERNIGHT LOOP

N

0   0.5   1.0
Mile

Hiker
Parking
Area

△
Cosby

ROUND
MOUNTAIN

Gabes Mountain Trail

INADU MOUNTAIN

Snake Den Ridge Trail

GABES MOUNTAIN

△
#34

Otter Creek

△
#29

x
3054 ft.

Old Settlers Trail

Albright Grove
Loop Trail

Maddron Bald Trail

Indian Camp Creek

*high-country creek near Maddron Bald, which sports awe-inspiring
views both above and below. On the return trip down the rugged Snake
Den Trail, a few more vistas open up on some smaller heath balds. This
excursion exemplifies the Smoky Mountains at their finest.*

Your trip starts on the Gabes Mountain Trail.
You'll cross several branches of Crying Creek on
footlogs before arriving at an old road turnaround at mile 1.1. While climbing the side of
Gabes Mountain, pass amid crumbling homesites

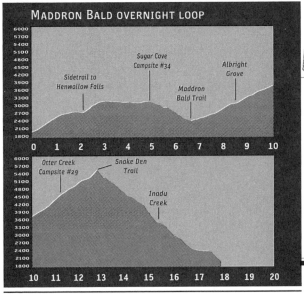

MADDRON BALD OVERNIGHT LOOP

Sidetrail to
Henwallow Falls

Sugar Cove
Campsite #34

Maddron
Bald Trail

Albright
Grove

Otter Creek
Campsite #29

Snake Den
Trail

Inadu
Creek

scattered in the second-growth woods along the
old road. A graded side trail leads to the foot of
Henwallow Falls at mile 2.1.

View the falls, then continue right on the
Gabes Mountain Trail to enter an old-growth
forest. Large, slick-surfaced beech trees and huge
hemlocks stand out among the giants. The trail
crosses small brooks that carve through the
mountainside and feed the fern and rhododendron understory.

Ford Greenbrier Creek at mile 4.8 and arrive
at Sugar Cove Backcountry Campsite #34 (elevation 3,240 feet). This is your first night's destination. The campsite gets a fair amount of use but is
in good shape, with camping areas lining the creek.

The next day, continue westward on the
Gabes Mountain Trail. Slowly snake your way
along Cole Creek; the trail crosses Cole Creek
and its tributaries so many times that you'll think
Cole Creek is the trail. Don't forget to look up at
all the big trees above as you rock-hop over the
watercourses. At mile 6.6, the trail arrives at the
Maddron Bald Trail junction.

Turn left up the Maddron Bald Trail, past the boulder in the middle of the road. Come to an old road turnaround at mile 7.7 of your loop hike. The trail becomes a rocky footpath, crossing Indian Camp Creek on a footlog at mile 8.2. The view up the creek is quite picturesque. Rounding the point of a small ridge, you'll come to the Albright Grove Nature Trail at mile 8.3.

Turn right on the nature trail and see some reasons for the establishment of this national park. Old-growth Carolina silverbells, hemlocks, beeches, and tulip trees have been spared the logger's axe and now enjoy national park protection along this 0.7-mile trail, which winds among the giants that lie between Indian Camp and Dunn creeks. Return to the Maddron Bald Trail at mile 9.0.

The Maddron Bald Trail ascends along, and sometimes through, Indian Camp and Copperhead creeks, leaving the cove to round the point of a ridge at mile 10.5. A small trail to your left emerges at a rocky overlook among crowded brush. From the overlook you can see the town of Cosby below. To your left is Snag Mountain. Up and to your right is Maddron Bald.

Keep ascending on the Maddron Bald Trail to reach Otter Creek Backcountry Campsite #29 (elevation 4,560 feet), at mile 11.0. This is your second night's destination. A small Civilian Conservation Corps camp once sat in this series of small level areas. A pulley-operated food hanging device, with directions, has been erected for your convenience. The wind rushes through the Otter Creek hollow throughout the year. Maddron Bald, a mere half-mile away, makes a good day hike from the camp.

Day three starts with the climb away from Otter Creek and up to Maddron Bald, reached at mile 11.5. This heath bald has low, dense bush cover rather than grass cover, but the occasional rock outcrop lets you take in the outstanding views, both near and far. The state-line ridge stands above and to the south; the lower Smokies and beyond extend north.

Beyond the bald, reenter the forest and intersect the Snake Den Ridge Trail at mile 12.5. This is the high point of the trip (elevation 5,800 feet), with telltale high-country spruce and fir trees about. Turn left on the Snake Den Ridge Trail and start working your way down a set of switchbacks. Occasionally, on the dry ridge tops, you'll be able to see over the heath-like groundcover to view the crest of the Smokies to your right.

At mile 15.2, the trail crosses Inadu Creek. It then works its way northeast down a cove to cross Rock Creek on a footlog at mile 16.2. Soon the trail comes into an old road turnaround and enters a previously settled area. A trail linking Snake Den Ridge Trail to the Low Gap Trail enters from the right at mile 16.8. Turn right and follow the connector trail 0.6 mile to the Low Gap Trail junction. Turn left and follow the Low Gap Trail 0.4 mile down to the hiker parking area at mile 17.8, completing the loop.

DIRECTIONS: From Gatlinburg, take US 321 east to a T intersection with TN 32. Turn right on TN 32 and follow it a little over 1 mile, turning right into the signed Cosby section of the park. At 2.1 miles on Cosby Road, arrive at the hiker parking area on the left, near the campground registration hut. Walk back on Cosby Road 0.1 mile to the picnic area. The Gabes Mountain Trail starts across the road from the picnic area.

Mount Sterling *Overnight Loop*

SCENERY: ✿ ✿ ✿ ✿ ✿

DIFFICULTY: ✿ ✿ ✿

TRAIL CONDITIONS: ✿ ✿ ✿ ✿

SOLITUDE: ✿ ✿ ✿ ✿

CHILDREN: ✿ ✿ ✿

DISTANCE: *5.1, 6.0, 6.2 miles each day*

HIKING TIME: *3:00, 4:00, 3:45 each day*

OUTSTANDING FEATURES: *Big Creek, Walnut Bottoms, views from Mount Sterling*

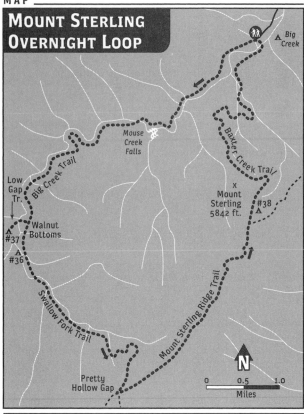

MOUNT STERLING OVERNIGHT LOOP

Start this trip at Big Creek Ranger Station (an out-of-the-way yet easily accessible departure point) for a trip along Big Creek and into the high country. Follow an old road on a gentle grade to Walnut Bottoms. Camp where several streams come together, providing ample fishing waters for those so inclined. Then climb the rigorous Swallow Fork Trail to the high country on Mount Sterling Ridge. Some pleasant ridge walking leads to Mount Sterling and your second night's destination, at the highest unsheltered backcountry campsite in the park. Pass through old growth forest on your descent along the Baxter Creek Trail back to Big Creek, where the loop ends.

🏃 Proceed up the Big Creek Trail past the gate and follow what was once a Native American footpath, then a logging railroad, and finally an auto road, until it returned to being a horse and footpath. Parallel Big Creek, an exceptionally attractive mountain stream, to pass the Rock House on the right at mile 1.0. Once home for logging

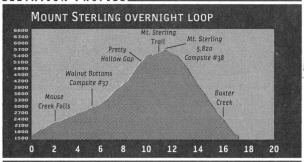

families until they could obtain better quarters, the Rock House provides shelter from the summer thunderstorms so prevalent in the Smokies.

Mouse Creek Falls spills into Big Creek on your left at mile 2.1. A wide Civilian Conservation Corps bridge spans Big Creek at mile 2.3. One of the Smokies' best-named and most famous springs appears on the left at mile 2.8. Brakeshoe Spring, christened for a railroad brake placed there by an engineer with a fondness for Smoky Mountain water, emerges on the left. The brake shoe is gone; only the name remains.

Continue following Big Creek as it horseshoes up the valley and then ford Flint Rock Cove Branch at mile 4.3. At mile 5.0, come to the Swallow Fork Trail junction. Stay on the Big Creek Trail and cross the bridge over Big Creek to enter Lower Walnut Bottoms Backcountry Campsite #37 (elevation 3,000 feet), at mile 5.1, your first night's destination. This campsite is popular among both hikers and bears. Food-storage boxes and hanging poles are provided to help keep the bears wild and hikers stocked with the provisions they brought. Do not leave food lying about.

Begin day two by crossing the bridge back over Big Creek and turning right on the Swallow Fork Trail at mile 5.2 of your loop hike. The ascent is on a gently graded trail until McGinty Creek, where it steepens considerably. At mile 6.0, the Swallow Fork Trail crosses Swallow Fork on a footlog. Cross McGinty Creek at mile 6.3, and after passing a mountain flat, begin the pull to reach Pretty Hollow Gap. Leave the Swallow Fork hollow and make a sharp right turn at mile 8.5 to switchback up to Pretty Hollow Gap. Here, at mile 9.2, the spruce-fir high country is nearly 1 mile in elevation.

Turn left on the Mount Sterling Ridge Trail, ascending out of the gap to a small knob flanked by fragrant evergreen trees. Briefly descend, then make the push for Mount Sterling. When you come to the Mount Sterling Trail junction at mile 10.6, pass straight through. The trail changes names at this point, from the Mount Sterling Ridge Trail to the Mount Sterling Trail. Pass through grassy and forested areas, then beyond a horse-hitch rack on your right, before topping out on Mount Sterling at mile 11.1.

A fire tower tops Mount Sterling, offering a 360-degree view. Be very careful on this or any other fire tower. Below the tower is Mount Sterling Backcountry Campsite #38 (elevation 5,800 feet). This is your second night's destination. To get water, descend the Baxter Creek Trail, which starts near the fire tower. At about 0.5 mile, look for a spur trail to a spring on trail left. Various designated campsites are sheltered among the evergreens below the fire tower. Note: The weather can be severe on Mount Sterling any time of the year.

Day three begins with a descent of the Baxter Creek Trail through old-growth forest that evokes the Canadian woods. Pass the trail to the spring at mile 11.6 of your loop hike. Switchbacks lead to and beyond the point of Mount Sterling Ridge at mile 13.3. The downgrade remains remarkably consistent until you enter the Baxter Creek valley, where you cross a branch of Baxter Creek at mile 15.6, and then cross Baxter Creek itself at mile 16.0. Continue along the east bank of Baxter Creek, crossing Big Creek on a footbridge before arriving at the Big Creek picnic area at mile 17.3, completing your loop.

DIRECTIONS: From Interstate 40, take exit 451, for Waterville. Cross the Pigeon River, then turn left to follow it upstream for 2.3 miles until you come to an intersection. Proceed forward through the intersection and soon enter the park. Pass the Big Creek Ranger Station and come to the Big Creek picnic area at mile 3.4. Park here and walk back on the road a short distance to the Big Creek trailhead.

Fork Ridge *Overnight Loop*

SCENERY: ✿ ✿ ✿ ✿ ✿
DIFFICULTY: ✿ ✿ ✿ ✿
TRAIL CONDITIONS: ✿ ✿ ✿
SOLITUDE: ✿ ✿ ✿ ✿
CHILDREN: ✿ ✿
DISTANCE: *5.2, 7.8, 6.7 miles each day*
HIKING TIME: *3:00, 4:45, 4:30 each day*
OUTSTANDING FEATURES: *big trees, diverse environments, views*

THIS TWO-NIGHT LOOP *is challenging, mainly due to elevation changes. Fortunately, the biggest climb is at the end, when your pack will be its lightest. Start on the seldom-traveled Fork Ridge Trail and amble underneath big spruce and yellow birch trees. Descend through several forest types before reaching Deep Creek Valley and Poke Patch Backcountry Campsite. Poke Patch is not as notable as the upcoming towering forests, but it will do. In the morning, continue descending in the attractive Deep Creek valley to reach the Pole Road Creek Trail. Climb to Noland Divide, only to drop down to Noland Creek on a rerouted section of pathway that leads to the Bald Creek campsite. On the final day, backtrack to Noland Divide, then climb into a spruce forest near Clingmans Dome Road. Follow the road briefly before intersecting the Appalachian Trail, then trace the A.T. back to Fork Ridge.*

🏃 Begin the overnight loop on the Fork Ridge Trail, descending in a brushy area. This trail is also part of the Mountains-to-Sea Trail, which accounts for the circular white blazes. Cruise along a narrow path with a broken overstory. At 0.7 mile, the trail levels and slips over to the left side of the ridge, in a red spruce woodland complemented by yellow birch, Fraser fir, witch hobble, and ferns aplenty. Pass a feeder stream of Keg Drive Branch at mile 1.4. Take notice of good views into the Deep Creek watershed. Grass

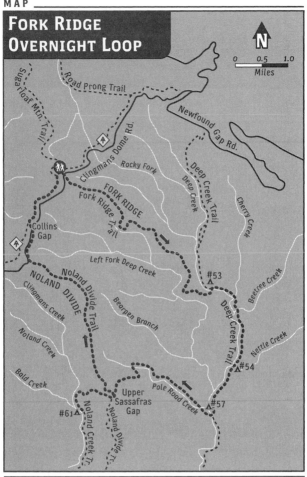

FORK RIDGE OVERNIGHT LOOP

N

0   0.5   1.0
Miles

Sugarloaf Mtn. Trail

Road Prong Trail

Newfound Gap Rd.

Clingmans Dome Rd.

Rocky Fork

FORK RIDGE

Fork Ridge Trail

Deep Creek Trail

Deep Creek

Cherry Creek

Collins Gap

Left Fork Deep Creek

#53

NOLAND DIVIDE

Noland Divide Trail

Clingmans Creek

Bearpen Branch

Deep Creek Trail

Beetree Creek

Noland Creek

Nettle Creek

Bald Creek

△#54

Upper Sassafras Gap

Pole Road Creek

#57

#61△

Noland Creek Tr.

Noland Divide Tr.

on the trail evidences the path's infrequent use. As the trail drops, cherry, beech, and hemlock trees appear in the forest.

Rejoin the crest of the ridge, where dry-environment species, such as chestnut oak, appear. There are views of Left Fork Deep Creek on the right. Starting at mile 3.8, the trail climbs a bit on the narrow ridgeline. Come to Deep Creek Gap at mile 4.6. The trail now makes an abrupt left turn and plunges toward Deep Creek. Just before reaching Deep Creek, look left at a switchback for a faint trail leading left 40 yards to a huge tulip tree. The circumference of this tree

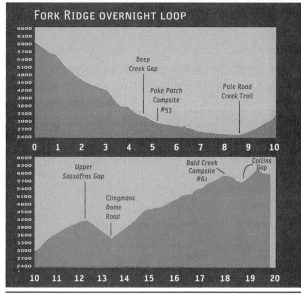

FORK RIDGE OVERNIGHT LOOP

Deep Creek Gap

Poke Patch Campsite #53

Pole Road Creek Trail

Upper Sassafras Gap

Clingmans Dome Road

Bald Creek Campsite #61

Collins Gap

amazes hikers willing to make the short detour. Return to the main trail and soon come to Deep Creek. This will be a wet crossing. Just across the stream, at 5.2 miles, are the junction with the Deep Creek Trail and Poke Patch Backcountry Campsite #53. The site, open to the sky overhead, has been in use for years and shows signs of wear. This is your first night's destination.

Start the second day by heading downstream on the Deep Creek Trail, which doubles as part of the Mountains-to-Sea Trail. Walk beneath a cathedral of more large trees. Around eye level, rhododendron and dog hobble grow. Deep Creek is sometimes seen, but always heard. At mile 5.9 of your loop hike, cross Cherry Creek. Climb away from the stream, only to drop back down among the rocks alongside Deep Creek. The trail here was blasted out of the mountainside. Beetree Creek comes in from your left. Keep descending through the rich valley and come to Nettle Creek Backcountry Campsite #54 at mile 7.8. Beyond this campsite, sycamores begin to appear in the forest. The trail opens to a flat with many white pines, reaching Pole Road Backcountry Campsite #57 at mile 8.7. Here you find a horse hitching post and picnic tables.

Just ahead, the path intersects the Pole Road Creek Trail. Here, turn right and cross Deep Creek on a two-part footbridge, high above the water. Soon, step over Pole Road Creek to ascend among more big trees, notably hemlock. Step over a couple of feeder streams, then cross Pole Road Creek again at 9.6 miles. The trail steepens a bit and crosses the stream again at miles 9.9, 10.2, 10.3, and, for the final time, at mile 10.9. The trail has been widened beyond this last crossing. Swing around a rib ridge of Noland Divide and keep ascending to reach Upper Sassafras Gap on Noland Divide at mile 12.0. Catch your breath at the gap, then drop into a rhododendron thicket, now on the Noland Creek Trail. The upper part of this path has been rerouted to ease the descent to Noland Creek, which lies at mile 12.8. Keep moving downstream along Noland Creek to reach Bald Creek Backcountry Campsite #61 at mile 13.0. This two-tiered campsite is your second night's destination. It must be reserved. The old, now closed, upper Noland Creek Trail is just downhill from the camp.

Start day three by backtracking to Noland Divide, reaching Upper Sassafras Gap at mile 14.0 of your loop hike. Turn left in an oak forest on the widening Noland Divide Trail and begin a steady climb to a small knob. Catch your breath on a level stretch in thickets of rhododendron after 14.5 miles. There are occasional views to the right of Burnt Spruce Ridge. As the climb resumes, enter a red spruce and yellow birch forest at mile 15.8. There are views of Forney Ridge to the left. Level out at 5,200 feet, then stairstep in a primeval woodland to reach a grassy road at mile 17.0. This closed road accesses a water source and acid-rain monitoring stations, one of which you will pass just ahead. Wind up the road in a frequently wet spruce-fir forest to reach Clingmans Dome Road at mile 17.7. Turn right here and walk the road for 0.7 mile, reaching the second of two gray stone walls on the right hand side of the road. At the second wall, turn left, cross Clingmans Dome Road, then dip into the woods to reach the Appalachian Trail at Collins Gap. If you come to a parking area on the right with 10 spaces in it, you have gone just a bit too far.

Once on the A.T., turn right, heading north. Climb out of Collins Gap and over Mount Collins, reaching 6,188 feet, then drop down to intersect the Sugarland Mountain Trail at mile 19.5. Stay on the A.T. and reach the Fork Ridge Connector Trail at mile 19.7. Turn right here and walk a few steps to Clingmans Dome Road, completing your loop.

> **DIRECTIONS**: From Newfound Gap, take Clingmans Dome Road for 3.5 miles to the Fork Ridge trailhead, which will be on your left.

Clingmans Dome
Overnight Loop

SCENERY: ✪ ✪ ✪ ✪ ✪
DIFFICULTY: ✪ ✪ ✪ ✪
TRAIL CONDITIONS: ✪ ✪ ✪ ✪
SOLITUDE: ✪ ✪ ✪
CHILDREN: ✪
DISTANCE: *6.7, 5.5, 12.8 miles each day*
HIKING TIME: *4:00, 2:45, 7:45 each day*
OUTSTANDING FEATURES: *views, attractive streams,
    multiple environments*

THIS LOOP STARTS *at the highest trailhead in the park, taking the Appalachian Trail past myriad views of the park and beyond. It then drops into Tennessee, where you leave the high-country spruce-fir forest for a streamside campsite in rich woodland that has everywhere-you-look beauty. Remain in the valley of the Little River for a lovely watershed walk, to spend your second night beneath Clingmans Dome at Three Forks. Get a good night's sleep here, as your final day makes a long and strenuous climb back to the high country via the Sugarland*

CLINGMANS DOME OVERNIGHT LOOP

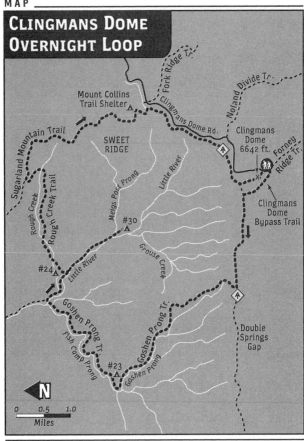

Mountain Trail, with more good views along the way. Finally, inter-sect the Appalachian Trail to undulate over Mount Collins and Cling-mans Dome. Make a final stop at the observation tower atop the dome before completing your loop.

🚶 Start your loop hike at the Clingmans Dome parking area, leaving on the Forney Ridge Trail through a spruce-fir forest. At 0.1 mile, veer right on the Clingmans Dome Bypass Trail. After a moderate half-mile climb, intersect the Appalachian Trail near Mount Buckley, elevation 6,500 feet. Continue west on the A.T., drop-ping through an area that bears the scars of fire. This section of trail offers impressive views, thanks to the low-lying recovering vegetation. Drop into a saddle, only to ascend again briefly,

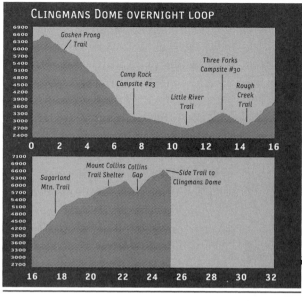

CLINGMANS DOME OVERNIGHT LOOP

topping a rock outcrop that makes a wonderful bench for gazing across North Carolina.

Enter again the spruce-fir forest, moving downward all the while. It is nearly always wet and cool here, pungent with the aroma of rich earth, of growing and decaying vegetation. After a brief level section, come to the Goshen Prong Trail at mile 2.7. Turn right here, and descend on a rocky path, entering Tennessee. Spruce and yellow birch dominate the woodland. There are good views of the Volunteer State. Pass a spring branch at mile 3.0. Rhododendron and Fraser fir line the path. Soon, come to an open area with many trees downed by the remnants of Hurricane Opal. Fire cherry trees are quickly growing up here.

At mile 3.8, the trail swings right, passing a slope of moss-covered rocks. Goshen Prong becomes audible by mile 4.8. Keep descending into the Goshen Prong watershed, soon passing a curious, three-foot-high cave. Follow a feeder stream of Goshen Prong, which forms a waterfall on a tilted rock face. Saddle alongside Goshen Prong at mile 5.4 to pick up an old railroad grade. The descent continues. Look near your feet for pieces of coal that once fired the engines of the railroad age. The path leaves the grade and is pinched between Goshen Prong on the left and a bluff on the right.

Enter a flat and come to a trail sign at mile 6.6. Turn right here, still on the Goshen Prong Trail, and soon come to the side trail, right, for Camp Rock Backcountry Campsite #23. Turn right and enter a yellow birch forest. The large camp has many level sites. Water can be obtained from Fish Camp Prong, just across the main path. This is your first night's destination.

Start your second day by continuing down the Goshen Prong Trail, immediately crossing onto an island of Fish Camp Prong. This is an exceptionally attractive valley, with yellow birch trees shading the pools and cascades of Fish Camp Prong. Occasional streamside flats and rock bluffs add scenic variation to the hike. At mile 7.1 of your loop hike, pass the old, now closed, Camp Rock campsite in an open flat to the left. Leave the railroad grade you have been following and climb away from the stream on a steep path, only to drop back down to Fish Camp Prong.

Come to an old traffic circle at mile 9.1. The center of the circle is now home to young trees. Keep treading down the widening valley to meet the Little River. An iron bridge spans the stream in the same location where a railroad bridge stood long ago. Head forward past the bridge and intersect the Little River Trail at mile 9.9. Turn right here and begin a moderate ascent on an old railroad grade, reaching the Rough Creek Backcountry Campsite #24 at mile 10.6. Keep forward and soon pass the Rough Creek Trail, which leaves left. Save this trail for tomorrow. Continue on the Little River Trail, crossing Meigs Post Prong at mile 11.8, where remnants of an old railroad bridge lie about the creek bed. Despite evidence of campers here, this is not a legal camping area. The real Three Forks campsite lies

ahead, reached after crossing what's left of the
Little River at mile 12.2, where another old
railroad bridge is evident. Three Forks Backcountry Campsite #30, which sits at an elevation
of 3,400 feet, was once a logging camp. This is
your second night's destination: a grassy area
surrounded by a birch forest, bounded on three
sides by high-country streams. Rest well, so you
will be prepared for a long day tomorrow.

Start day three by backtracking 1.6 miles down
the Little River Trail to the Rough Creek Trail,
at mile 13.8 of your loop hike. Turn right and
begin climbing through second-growth forest
dominated by tulip trees. Cross Rough Creek at
mile 14.3, then turn well away from the watercourse. Descend to cross the stream again at mile
15.1, then cross a third time. Get water here—this is
the last source for several miles. Ascend the
slope of Sugarland Mountain, passing through
hemlock coves. Rock work on the downside of the
trail keeps the path level. Reach the Sugarland
Mountain Trail at mile 16.6. Turn right here and
keep climbing on a knife-edge ridge. Eventually,
the trail stays primarily on the west side of the
ridge, affording views into Tennessee.

Pass by occasional rock outcrops. At 17.1
miles, the trail straddles a piney ridge. There are
great views to the right of Sweet Ridge, Miry
Ridge, and Blanket Mountain in the distance.
Red spruce trees begin to appear, indicating this
is high country—in fact, you are now 5,000 feet
above sea level. Yellow birch with widespread
crowns complement the stately spruce trees.
Climb to meet Sweet Ridge and keep pushing on,
passing the Mount Collins Trail Shelter Spring at
mile 20.8. Intersect the side trail to the shelter.
The Sugarland Mountain Trail levels, then makes
a short climb in spruce-fir woods to meet the
Appalachian Trail at mile 21.4. Turn right on the
A.T. for a brief climb over Mount Collins and
then descend, reaching Collins Gap at 22.6
miles. Climb away from Collins Gap and wind up

to Clingmans Dome. The trailside vegetation is a hodgepodge of brush, grass, and trees. Come to the side trail for Clingmans Dome tower at 24.5 miles. Turn left here and soon reach the observation tower. From here, descend on a paved path to complete your loop at 25 miles.

DIRECTIONS: From Newfound Gap, drive 7 miles to the end of Clingmans Dome Road. The Forney Ridge Trail starts at the end of the Clingmans Dome parking area.

Newton Bald *Overnight Loop*

SCENERY: ✿ ✿ ✿ ✿
DIFFICULTY: ✿ ✿ ✿
TRAIL CONDITIONS: ✿ ✿ ✿ ✿
SOLITUDE: ✿ ✿ ✿
CHILDREN: ✿ ✿
DISTANCE: *6.3, 7.0, 9.8 miles each day*
HIKING TIME: *4:00, 4:45, 5:30 each day*
OUTSTANDING FEATURES: *history, Deep Creek, ridge walking*

O**N THIS TRIP,** *you'll head up the famed fishing waters of Deep Creek, the origin of many a Smoky Mountain hunting and fishing tale, to camp at a streamside site on a carpet of pine needles beneath a grove of white pines. You will leave the Deep Creek watershed via the steep Martins Gap Trail, then intersect the Sunkota Ridge Trail for some nice ridge walking to a little-used Backcountry Campsite, 5,000 feet high on Thomas Ridge. Finally, the loop heads south on the ridge, following the Thomas Divide Trail back to Deep Creek.*

🏃 Begin the hike on the Deep Creek Trail, which starts out as a gravel road, passing the Indian Creek Trail junction at mile 0.7. Cross Indian Creek on a bridge and continue up Deep Creek Trail to a road turnaround at mile 2.2, crossing three bridges and passing the Loop Trail junction along the way. Leave the road to follow a graded trail that traverses Bumgardner Branch, and arrive at Bumgardner Branch Backcountry Campsite #60, at mile 2.9. Stay on the east bank of Deep Creek, which rises far above the creek itself. An historic wagon road once intersected the creek here.

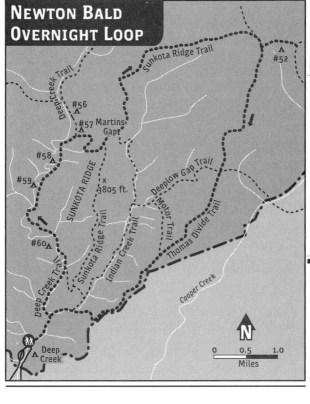

NEWTON BALD OVERNIGHT LOOP

Drop down to McCracken Branch Backcountry Campsite #59, at mile 4.2. Repeat the pattern of rise and fall to enter Nicks Nest Branch Backcountry Campsite #58, at mile 5.7. Trace the right bank of Deep Creek, coming to the historic Bryson Place and a trail junction at mile 6.0. Once the site of a backwoods cabin and a hunting lodge, this was a favorite haunt of famed outdoor writer and national park proponent Horace Kephart. Of course, fishing continues to be a recreational pastime of many Smokies visitors, as it was in his day.

Leave Bryson Place on the Deep Creek Trail and come to Burnt Spruce Backcountry Campsite #56 (elevation 2,405 feet), at mile 6.3. Spend your first night here, under the big white pines,

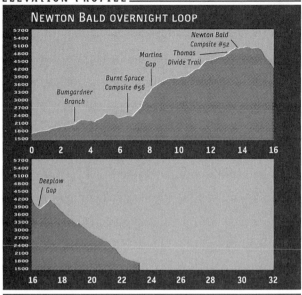

with Deep Creek rushing nearby. This campsite is nestled between two others that receive heavier usage, Bryson Place and Pole Road; thus it remains a quiet creekside camp.

Day two begins by returning to Bryson Place, 0.3 mile back down the Deep Creek Trail. Turn left up the Martins Gap Trail, climbing a steep 1.5 miles to its namesake gap at mile 8.1 of your loop hike. Turn left on the infrequently trodden Sunkota Ridge Trail, gently ascending out of Martins Gap around the east side of a knob. Continue ascending, passing a spring at mile 9.5. The trail promises to top out, yet it keeps gaining elevation in moderate spurts between level areas to intersect the Thomas Divide Trail at mile 12.9 (elevation 4,780 feet).

Turn right on the Thomas Divide Trail and walk 0.4 mile to arrive at the Newton Bald Trail junction. Turn left on the Newton Bald Trail, following it 0.1 mile to the Newton Bald Back-country Campsite #52, your second night's desti-nation. This 5,000-foot-high campsite, located in a saddle on Thomas Divide near what was once an open meadow, is a pleasant place to escape the summer heat and crowds. In the winter, Newton Bald is susceptible to strong winds. Chestnut trees still grow on this former bald, but they don't get very big; after a few year's growth, they succumb to the same chestnut blight that essentially wiped out the Smokies' most prolific food-bearing tree species in the 1920s.

Start day three by backtracking 0.1 mile to the Thomas Divide Trail. Turn left and begin a southwesterly course toward Deep Creek Ranger Station. Walk among wooded knolls around 5,000 feet in elevation for nearly 2 miles, then begin a prolonged descent, passing the Deeplow Gap Trail at mile 16.5 of your loop hike. Climb out of Deeplow Gap and begin an undulating course on the ridge.

At mile 18.9, intersect what was once the Indian Creek Motor Nature Trail, begun in the 1960s but halted due to public outcry. The roadbed, running parallel to the park boundary, makes for easy walking as you continually lose elevation. Still on the Thomas Divide Trail, come to a trail junction at mile 21.0. Turn right on the Stone Pile Gap Trail and continue your descent, zigzagging over the small creek that often muddies the trail.

Intersect the Indian Creek Trail at mile 22.0 and turn left. Pass by Indian Creek Falls on your right, then come to another trail junction at mile 22.4. Turn left on the Deep Creek Trail and follow it 0.7 mile to complete your 23.1-mile loop.

DIRECTIONS: From the Oconaluftee Visitor Center, take US 441 south to Cherokee, North Carolina. Turn right on US 19 and drive 10 miles to Bryson City, North Carolina. Turn right at the Swain County Courthouse onto Everett Street and carefully follow the signs through town to the Deep Creek campground. The Deep Creek Trail is at the back of the campground.

Springhouse Branch
Overnight Loop

SCENERY: ✿ ✿ ✿ ✿
DIFFICULTY: ✿ ✿
TRAIL CONDITIONS: ✿ ✿ ✿ ✿
SOLITUDE: ✿ ✿ ✿
CHILDREN: ✿ ✿ ✿
DISTANCE: *5.4, 10.4, 7.2 miles each day*
HIKING TIME: *3:00, 5:30, 4:00 each day*
OUTSTANDING FEATURES: *history, creekside environment, virgin forest*

IF YOU ENJOY THE MAGIC *of an ever-changing Smoky Moun-tain stream, this trip is for you. Hike north into the Noland Creek watershed, passing several old homesites, to camp at Jerry Flats. Then take the Springhouse Branch Trail through virgin forest on Forney Ridge to the Forney Creek watershed, passing an old Civilian Conservation Corps camp. Continue up Forney Creek to camp where Jonas Creek flows into Forney Creek. Return along Forney Creek to the Whiteoak Branch Trail, then exit at the end of the "Road to Nowhere" through an abandoned tunnel.*

🚶 Start your trip at the lower end of the Noland Creek parking area. Follow this short trail down to the Noland Creek Trail. Turn right on the Noland Creek Trail, passing under the Noland Creek bridge on Lakeview Drive, then over a bridge spanning Noland Creek at mile 0.3. Continue up the old road, passing the side trail to Bear Pen Branch Backcountry Campsite #65, at mile 1.3 on the Noland Creek Trail.

Cross cascading Noland Creek on a second bridge in an area of old homesites at mile 1.9. Look around for the remaining stone foundations and chimneys. Span Noland Creek on wide bridges at miles 2.7 and 4.0. You are now in the Solola Valley, which housed enough people to warrant its own school. Mill Creek Backcountry Campsite #64, at mile 4.2, is used primarily by horse campers.

To the left is the Springhouse Branch Trail. Veer right and stay on the Noland Creek Trail, immediately crossing Noland Creek on a footlog. After the crossing you'll spot an abandoned

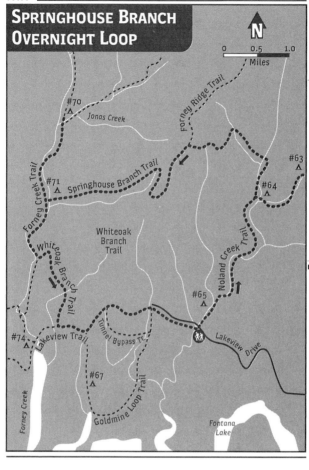

SPRINGHOUSE BRANCH OVERNIGHT LOOP

ranger station, nearly hidden among the trees. Continue the moderate ascension up the right bank of Noland Creek to cross the creek once more on a footlog at mile 5.0. After another 0.4 mile, come upon Jerry Flats Backcountry Camp-site #63 (elevation 2,920 feet). This is your first night's destination. The campsite is flat and fairly open, probably an old homesite.

After a night in Jerry Flats, start day two by backtracking down Noland Creek Trail 1.2 miles, to intersect the Springhouse Branch Trail at mile 6.6 of your loop hike. Turn right on the Spring-house Branch Trail, immediately crossing Mill Creek twice among the rhododendron. At mile

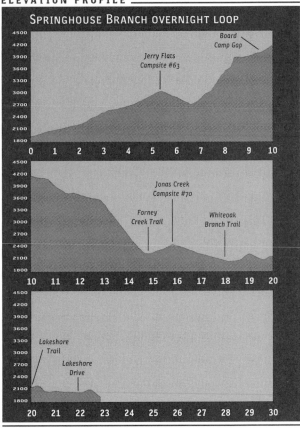

SPRINGHOUSE BRANCH OVERNIGHT LOOP

7.1, rock piles, washtubs, and an old chimney are evidence of pre-park settlement in this interesting area. Turn westward after crossing Mill Creek on a footlog, still in previously settled country.

Ascend along Springhouse Branch and enter virgin woods, crossing small feeder streams in the mountain cove before winding around the point of a ridge at mile 8.4. Work up the side of Forney Ridge and come to Board Camp Gap and a trail junction at mile 9.4. An old shack of rough-hewn boards once stood here, giving the gap its name.

Climb southward out of the gap, staying on the Springhouse Branch Trail, turning away from Rough Hew Ridge. After a switchback, turn north and cross Bee Gum Branch at mile 11.1. Begin

descending on the north side of Bee Gum
Branch hollow. Two prominent switchbacks
signal your imminent arrival at Forney Creek.
After crossing Bee Gum Branch, pass through
CCC Backcountry Campsite #71, to intersect
the Forney Creek Trail at mile 14.8. Turn right
onto the Forney Creek Trail and pass amid
Civilian Conservation Corps relics such as
barrels, a chimney, even an old bathtub. Beyond
the campsite, climb a hill, then drop to the creek
again. Pass Locust Cove Branch and come to the
Jonas Creek Trail junction at mile 15.8.

Turn left on the Jonas Creek Trail and
immediately cross Forney Creek on a long footlog. Just beyond a rhododendron thicket is Jonas
Creek Backcountry Campsite #70 (elevation
2,400 feet). This is your second night's destination. Jonas and Forney creeks, on either side of
the large, level campsite backed up against a steep
hill, will sing you to sleep as night falls.

Start day three by crossing Forney Creek and
backtracking to the Forney Creek Trail. Turn
right on the Forney Creek Trail and return to
CCC Backcountry Campsite, at mile 16.8 of your
loop hike. Continue along the creek to climb the
side of a hill, avoiding the tough fords of the old
Forney Creek Trail. Drop to the crashing stream,
only to climb once again. Intersect the Whiteoak
Branch Trail at mile 18.0. Turn left on the
Whiteoak Branch Trail, crossing Whiteoak
Branch to top out in a gap. As you begin
descending, signs of human presence appear
along Gray Wolf Creek. Turn left away from an
old road that parallels Gray Wolf Creek and
intersect the Lakeshore Trail in an old homesite
clearing at mile 20.0.

Turn left on the Lakeshore Trail and begin
ascending along a rill over a gap leading to the
Goldmine Loop Trail junction at mile 21.5.
Continue on the Lakeshore Trail at this intersection and again at at junction with the Tunnel
Bypass Trail. Continue another 0.5 mile to the
tunnel that was the final project of the "Road to

Nowhere," a failed 1940s attempt to build an additional paved road through the park. Once in the tunnel, let your eyes adjust to the dimness, and you'll see the light at the tunnel's end. When outside again, enter the parking area at the end of Lakeview Drive, the official name of the "Road to Nowhere." A less-than-ideal walk along 0.7 mile of road leads to the Noland Creek parking area, the loop's end.

> **DIRECTIONS:** From the Oconaluftee Visitor Center, head south on Newfound Gap Road for 3.2 miles to US 19 in Cherokee, North Carolina. Turn right on US 19 and follow it 10 miles to Bryson City, North Carolina. Once in Bryson City, turn right at the courthouse and continue straight on Everett Street, which becomes Lakeview Drive. The Noland Creek parking area is on the left, 5 miles beyond the park border.

Gregory Bald *Overnight Loop*

SCENERY: ✪ ✪ ✪ ✪ ✪
DIFFICULTY: ✪ ✪ ✪
TRAIL CONDITIONS: ✪ ✪ ✪ ✪
SOLITUDE: ✪ ✪ ✪ ✪
CHILDREN: ✪ ✪
DISTANCE: *4.1, 4.6, 7.0 miles each day*
HIKING TIME: *2:30, 3:00, 4:00*
OUTSTANDING FEATURES: *good campsites, high country meadows*

THIS HIKE COMBINES *the best that the high and low country have to offer. First, you'll travel the Twentymile Trail past Twentymile Cascades to the Upper Flats streamside camp. Then an arduous climb tops out on Long Hungry Ridge and leads to the Gregory Bald Trail, arriving at the most famous bald in southern Appalachia, with its staggering views and flower displays. Camp at Sheep Pen Gap, a high-country grassy glade between Gregory Bald and Parson Bald. Leave the grassy balds and complete your loop via the steep Wolf Ridge Trail.*

🚶 Start your hike on the Twentymile Trail, following it to the Wolf Ridge Trail junction at mile 0.6. Turn right, passing the side trail to Twentymile Cascades on your right at mile 0.7. Climb moderately, passing over Twentymile Creek on wide bridges at miles 1.4 and 1.6. Just beyond the

MAP

THE BACKCOUNTRY

&OVERNIGHT
DAY
HIKES

part three

GREAT OVERNIGHT LOOPS

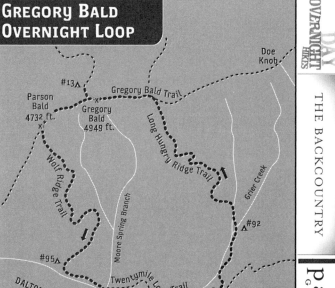

GREGORY BALD OVERNIGHT LOOP

Doe Knob

#13△

Gregory Bald Trail

Parson Bald
4732 ft.

Gregory Bald
4949 ft.

Long Hungry Ridge Trail

Grier Creek

Wolf Ridge Trail

△#92

#95△

Moore Spring Branch

Twentymile Loop Trail

DALTON RIDGE

Wolf Ridge Trail

#93△

Twentymile Trail

TWENTYMILE RIDGE

Twentymile
Ranger Station

Cheoah Lake

N

0   0.5   1.0
Miles

ELEVATION PROFILE

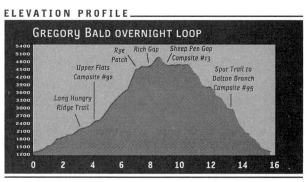

GREGORY BALD OVERNIGHT LOOP

5400
5100
4800
4500
4200
3900
3600
3300
3000
2700
2400
2100
1800
1500
1200

Rye Patch

Rich Gap

Sheep Pen Gap
Campsite #13

Upper Flats
Campsite #92

Spur Trail to
Dalton Branch
Campsite #95

Long Hungry
Ridge Trail

0   2   4   6   8   10   12   14   16

second crossing is Twentymile Creek Backcountry
Campsite #93. Cross another bridge at the back
of the campsite. The trail climbs above the creek,

then drops down and crosses Twentymile Creek twice more on bridges, before coming to Proctor Gap at mile 3.0.

Stay forward on the old railroad bed and pick up the Long Hungry Ridge Trail, crossing Proctor Creek at mile 3.1. Swing around the point of a ridge, then come alongside Twentymile Creek again. The rotting bridges on the side streams are remnants of the logging era, in which railroads were built to haul timber. These bridges are dangerous! Do not try to use them to cross the creek. At mile 4.1, come to Upper Flats Backcountry Campsite #92 (elevation 2,520 feet). This is your first night's destination. Upper Flats has several good tent sites. Large rocks emerge from the ground, forming natural seats at the campsite.

Start day two by immediately crossing Twenty-mile Creek, then Rye Patch Branch. The once-moderate grade becomes steep as the trail crosses Rye Patch Branch at mile 4.6 of your loop hike. It then ascends the dry hillside. After a sharp right turn, come to Rye Patch (elevation 4,500 feet) at mile 6.8. This formerly open area is rapidly growing over but still remains an ideal resting spot after you've made the climb to the crest of Long Hungry Ridge.

Now atop the ridge, the last 0.8 mile of the Long Hungry Ridge Trail is easy, ending at the Gregory Bald Trail junction at mile 7.6. Turn left on the Gregory Bald Trail, coming soon to Rich Gap and another trail junction at mile 7.7. If you are thirsty, turn left on the unmarked side trail and go 0.3 mile to Moore Spring, site of an old Appalachian Trail shelter. From Rich Gap, continue forward on the Gregory Bald Trail and climb 0.6 mile to the grassy meadow of Gregory Bald at mile 8.3. The bald, maintained at its present 15-acre size by the park service, offers a nearly 360-degree view. Flame azaleas bloom in June and blueberries follow.

Reenter the woods on the western end of the bald and descend to the Wolf Ridge Trail junction and Sheep Pen Gap Backcountry Campsite

#13 (elevation 4,560 feet), at mile 8.7. This is your second night's destination, a grassy glade of open, level woodland—one of the Smokies' finest backcountry campsites. You can find water at a spring 200 yards down the Gregory Bald Trail, on your left. Sunset from atop Gregory Bald is a Smoky Mountain sight not to be missed.

Start day three by heading southwest on the Wolf Ridge Trail through level woodland with a grassy ground cover. Come to Parson Bald at mile 9.5 of your loop hike. This bald, unlike Gregory Bald, is not maintained by the park service and is rapidly filling with trees and bushes, which limit views. But look over your left shoulder as you enter the clearing to view grassy Gregory Bald. Leave the bald and continue on a nearly level hike for another 0.8 mile, then begin an intermittent, but steep descent down Wolf Ridge.

Swing right toward Dalton Branch, coming to the side trail leading to Dalton Branch Backcountry Campsite #95, at mile 13.1. Veer left beyond the campsite and pick up an old road that descends steeply to the Twentymile Loop Trail junction at mile 14.1. Ford Moore Spring Branch at miles 14.2 and 14.4. In the next 0.7 mile, cross Moore Spring Branch three times on footlogs to arrive at the Twentymile Trail junction at mile 15.1. Cross Moore Spring Branch a final time just beyond the junction and follow the Twentymile Trail 0.6 mile to the trailhead, completing your loop.

DIRECTIONS: From Townsend, Tennessee, take US 321 north to the Foothills Parkway. Follow Foothills Parkway west to US 129. Follow US 129 south into North Carolina. Turn left on NC 28. Follow NC 28 for 2.6 miles to the Twentymile Ranger Station, on your left. Park beyond the ranger station and walk up to the gated road and begin your hike on the Twentymile Trail. From the courthouse in Bryson City, North Carolina, take US 19 south for 5.4 miles to NC 28. Follow NC 28 for 30 miles to reach the Twentymile Ranger Station, on your right.

Index